BURT FRANKLIN: RESEARCH & SOURCE WORKS SERIES
Selected Studies in History, Economics, & Social Science:
n.s. 38,(c) Modern European Studies.

LETTERS

CONCERNING THE

ENGLISH NATION.

VOLTAIRE

LETTERS

CONCERNING THE

ENGLISH

NATION.

WITH AN INTRODUCTION

BY CHARLES WHIBLEY.

BURT FRANKLIN REPRINTS
New York, N. Y.

914.2035
V88L
94785
Oct 1975

Published by LENOX HILL Pub. & Dist. Co. (Burt Franklin)
235 East 44th St., New York, N.Y. 10017
Reprinted: 1974
Printed in the U.S.A.

Burt Franklin: Research and Source Works Series
Selected Studies in History, Economics, and Social Science: n.s. 38,(c)
  Modern European Studies.

Reprinted from the original edition in the University of Minnesota
  Library.

Library of Congress Cataloging in Publication Data

Voltaire, Francois Marie Arouet de, 1694-1778.
  Letters concerning the English nation.

  At head of title: Voltaire.
  Reprint of the 1926 ed. published by P. Davies, London.
  Translation of Lettres philosophiques.
  1. Great Britain—Intellectual life—18th century. 2. Great Britain—Religion.
3. English literature—18th century—History and criticism. I. Title.
PQ2086.L4E5 1974   914.2'03'5   74-728
ISBN 0-8337-4467-4

INTRODUCTION.

V OLTAIRE *arrived in England at a moment of good fortune. It was a fine day in May, and the sun was shining. A west wind blew upon the banks of the Thames, and Greenwich appeared to his stranger's eye a place of enchantment.* Nothing was lacking that might delight the eye and the ear of the traveller. The white-sailed ships, the music, which accompanied the King and Queen in their gilded barge, the race-course, the men and women on horseback, the young girls afoot, the quick movement and the gay laughter*

---

* There was a time when London could be approached without disgust of the remoter suburbs, and the first impressions of old travellers were commonly happy. Erasmus does not yield to Voltaire in enthusiasm. " Did you but know the blessings of Britain, you would clap wings to your feet, and run hither; and if the gout stopped you, would wish yourself a Daedalus." Thus writes Erasmus to Faustus Andrelinus, to whom he particularly commended " one attraction out of many; there are nymphs here with divine features, so gentle and kind, that you may well prefer them to your Camenae. . . . Wherever you go you are received on all hands with kisses. . . . O Faustus, if you had once tasted how sweet and how fragrant these kisses are, you would wish to be a traveller, not for ten years, like Solon, but for your whole life, in England."

*persuaded him that he was in a country of legend. Were not these the Olympic games? And did not Greenwich Park far exceed in beauty the plain of Elis? The same day he went to Court, where he was instantly disillusioned. There the ladies, stiff and cold in manner, read the gazette or played at quadrille, and when they condescended to notice his presence, they put him out of humour by telling him that he had wasted his enthusiasm at Greenwich on a parcel of apprentices, mounted on hired nags. On the morrow he was still more bitterly discomfited. The friends, who at Greenwich had received him with a watchful kindness, passed him by, as though they knew him not. Had he offended them, he wondered; and he presently discovered that their ill-humour came from nothing else than the East Wind. As he went further on his way, he was told that Molly, a rich and beautiful girl, on the eve of her marriage had cut her throat, and when he asked why, he was told: the wind is in the East. The East Wind also explained the gloom which hung over the Court, and he made up his mind that never would he ask a favour there, save when the wind was in the West or in the South.**

S o *Voltaire pricked with the needle of his irony the surface of things, as they presented themselves to him in England. His eye was quick to discover the inconsistences and contrasts of English life. When he saw a man, who yesterday had bragged of*

* See letter A M. ****, printed in Vol. xxii, p. 18 of Moland's Edition of Voltaire.

his liberty, to-day the prisoner of the press-gang, his sense of incongruity was touched. But it was not for him to stay his hand at the surface ; there was knowledge to acquire in England, and he meant to acquire it. He deeply deplored the ignorance of England and things English, which he observed in Paris. And this ignorance was one-sided. English ministers in France speak and read French, said he, who had known Prior. A French Ambassador in London, he confessed, generally knows not a word of English. How, then should the one country be revealed to the other? " If you want light "—such was Voltaire's conclusion— " you must rely upon a private citizen, who has assez de loisir et d'opiniâtreté *to learn English." Voltaire had both* loisir et opiniâtreté, *and he studied English to such purpose that he cast a glimmer, obscured by occasional patches of dark-ness, upon England and the English, and that glimmer has guided the French through their night of ignorance ever since.*

V O L T A I R E *had friends among the great in England before he visited it, and without difficulty he added to the number. His easy manners, too easy some called them, the rumours which followed him from Paris, his tireless curiosity opened many doors to him. But it was not among the great that he sought the retirement, in which he might give his days to study. He visited Bolingbroke and Pope and Swift. He found tranquillity in the house of the admirable Everard Falkener, merchant and* *man of affairs. In Falkener's quiet retreat at Wandsworth, he made himself master of the English tongue; and he retained something of that mastery until the end of his life. Truly the years which Voltaire spent in England were not years of idleness. It may be doubted whether he was ever idle. He published a couple of essays in English, that he might furnish forth a proof of his knowledge of our language; he sent forth his noble edition of the* Henriade, *with its noble list of subscribers and its dedication to the Queen. He collected material for his* History of Charles XII *in London, where alone he could have collected it, and he wrote his celebrated* Letters Concerning the English Nation,* *which he published in English in* 1733, *and in France a year later under the title of* Lettres Philosophiques.

T H E *book was received in London with universal applause. The Abbé Prévost in* Le Pour et le Contre (1733) *is witness that* " *persons of the highest distinction urged the printers to haste." The Court and the Town were equally enthusiastic. Many were astonished that they should have made their first appearance in English, and it was*

---

* The *Letters* were translated into English by John Lockman, an industrious hack, who had learned French by frequenting Slaughter's Coffee House, whither Johnson followed him, for a like purpose and with less success. Lockman translated also *L'Henriade*. He was something of a poet, and being also Secretary to the British Herring Fishery presented at Court both verses and pickled herrings. They were received with equal graciousness.

rumoured that the English version was the true original. To this rumour the Abbé Prévost gave a flat contradiction. " I know," said he, " that the original is French, and that the translator is Mr. Lockman." He had himself seen the French copy, and though he admits that the translation sometimes deforms the author's meaning, he esteems it scarcely inferior to the original. At any rate, it met with a far more amicable reception in England than that which awaited it a year later in its native France.

THIS book was the chief of the spoils won by Voltaire in England. It is light in hand, wayward and amusing. If it does not penetrate very deeply into the truth, it gives proof of Voltaire's wide interest and quick understanding. It makes no pretence to cover the whole ground or to exhaust this subject or that. Voltaire chooses such topics to write about as suited the whim of the moment, and his choice was guided now and again by the hope of castigating France, while he described England. He keeps always a suspicious and ironic eye upon his own country. That is why he gives the pride of place and of length also to a dissertation upon the Quakers. There was little in the Quakers to engross Voltaire's sceptical mind save their novelty and their complete alienation from the spirit of France. That he had a certain sympathy with them is clear ; it is clear also that his sympathy would have been less warmly expressed, had he not known that in praising the Quakers he was defying the *authority of his own country. As he understood the Quaker doctrine it was a vindication of liberty. And of liberty—the only liberty worth having— the liberty to live and to think, as you like, Voltaire was always a gallant champion. For the many sorts of liberty which have been cherished since his time, he would have had no respect. He would have thought little of the liberty which is interpreted by the right to vote, or of the liberty which claims the right of disturbing others by its loud expression. But he saw that the English enjoyed privileges, which he thought desirable, and which were denied to Frenchmen, and he did not hesitate to applaud their freedom.*

" ENGLAND," he said, " is properly the land of sectarists. Multae sunt mansiones in domo patris mei (in my father's house are many mansions). *An Englishman, as one to whom liberty is natural, may go to heaven his own way." He presently gave the thought a sharper turn, when he said that England had thirty religions and only one sauce. And he freely owned that the multiplication of sects had its uses. " If one religion only were allowed in England," said he, " the government would very possibly become arbitrary; if there were but two, the people would cut one another's throats; but as there is such a multitude, they all live happy and in peace." His curiosity about strange religions, then, induced him to admire the Quakers, further removed than any others from his own Catholicism. The visit which he paid to Mr. Andrew Pitt, the*

Quaker of Hampstead, " a hale ruddy-complexioned old man," afforded him much entertainment. He pretended to be shocked that the excellent Quaker had never been christened, and was " absolutely for forcing him " to the font. He listened in appreciative silence when Andrew Pitt told him that it was " to secure themselves more strongly from such a shameless traffick of lies and flattery, that they thee'd *and* thou'd *a king with the same freedom as we do a beggar, and saluted no person," and he allowed the old gentleman to carry him off to a Quaker's meeting.*

I F *Voltaire took pleasure in contemplating the independence of Andrew Pitt and other sectaries, he wondered with an equal pleasure at the esteem in which men of science and letters were held in England. He observed that the monuments set up to men of genius in Westminster Abbey raised the admiration of spectators more readily than the tombs of kings. He liked to remember that the greatest men in England disputed who should hold up Sir Isaac Newton's pall. But his respect for the English was never so loudly expressed as when he records the honour that was done to the actress, Mrs. Oldfield, when she was interred in the Abbey of Westminster. It had been said in France that the funeral honours of the state had been paid the actress to make the French more sensible of their barbarity in dumping the body of Adrienne le Couvreur ignominiously in the fields. He assured his countrymen that " the English were prompted by no other Principle, in burying Mrs. Oldfield in Westminster Abbey, than their own good sense."*

VOLTAIRE *was always a gallant champion of his craft. No man was ever prouder of the title of poet and man of letters than he. When he saw Newton treated, after death: " as a king who had made his people happy," he snatched one leaf of the laurels, which Newton had won, for his own head. It was for this reason that he misunderstood the pride and aloofness from his art of Congreve. The encounter is familiar to all, and it is clear that the two men failed to understand one another. In Voltaire's eyes, the one defect of Congreve was that he entertained " too mean an idea of his first profession." Indeed, he hinted to Voltaire at their first meeting, that Voltaire " should visit him on no other foot than that of a gentleman , who led a life of plainness and simplicity." Voltaire's retort was obvious—that had Congreve been so unfortunate as to be a mere gentleman he would not have come to see him. Yet Voltaire had the worst of the encounter. Congreve, being a reticent Englishman, disliked to wear the professional label of a writer. His plays were but a memory to him, and the society, which he had studied that he might depict it, meant, in his mature years, more for him than the craft which he had practised conspicuously well. It was his nature, as Giles Jacob said " not to show so much the poet as the gentleman ", and Voltaire, who clung to the official uniform of the Muses, professed to be shocked.*

L I K E *many of his countrymen, then and since, Voltaire, ever ready to fight for liberty in life and politics, would permit no freedoms in literature. He was passive in obedience to the traditions of his art. He would not swerve a hand's breadth from the ordinances of tradition. He did not permit his eye to wander at large over the field of letters. When literature was his quest, he put a check upon his curiosity, which he was free to exercise if it were merely life and politics that engrossed him.* He came to England with the rules of Aristotle and others neatly arranged in his brain. He was convinced that nobody could be a poet, who did not obey the laws which had been drawn up in the past, who did not revere the unities, and who did not bow the knee before the twin deities of good taste and good sense. He would have been indignant if he had heard Dryden's comment that " the affected purity of the French had unsinewed their language." Between Dryden and Voltaire, truly, there could not have been complete sympathy. Much as he admired Dryden, Voltaire found his genius " too exuberant, and not accompanied with judgment enough." His approval of Pope was whole-hearted, as we might expect. Pope was the most elegant, the most correct, the most harmonious poet, that England had ever given birth to. Rochester was for*

---

* No better instance can be given of this strange opposition than the practice of the late Anatole France, Voltaire's devout disciple, who, a violent Jacobin in politics, was ever a fierce anti-Jacobin in literature.

Voltaire, as he should be, a man of genius. And Addison was the master of all, to whose standard of taste it became men and poets to aspire. If only Shakespeare had been Addison's contemporary, and had learned the lessons which he taught, what a dramatist he would have been! He might have written a play as good as Cato.

FIRMLY *as he clings in general to his rules of taste and sense, Voltaire now and again seems to loosen his hold. His admiration of Butler is a sudden surprise. To say of* Hudibras, *as he does,* " I never found so much wit in any one single book as that," *is to be false to his own doctrine. Many, indeed, are the merits of* Hudibras, *but among these merits I would not place good sense and good taste. However, Voltaire admits that it is untranslatable and that it would need a commentary to explain it. And who but a blockhead would* " set up for a commentator of smart sayings and repartees? " *His respect for Swift is more easily intelligible. In expression, at any rate, Swift adheres closely to the rules. He is a classic, scrupulous in the choice and parsimonious in the use of words. And the two men had met upon terms of intimacy. Voltaire had given Swift letters of introduction, when Swift contemplated a journey to Paris, and Swift had promised, and had surely carried out his promise, to find subscribers for the* Henriade *in Dublin. Yet as you read his appreciation of Swift, you cannot but think that he is using Swift as a rod with which to chastise Rabelais. For Voltaire Swift is* " Rabelais

in his senses, and frequenting the politest company "
(dans son bon sens et vivant en bonne com-
pagnie). " *Rabelais in his senses* " *is not so close
to wit or to the truth as Coleridge's* anima Rabelaisii
habitans in sicco, *than which no better definition
is likely to be found. But Voltaire, the anti-revolu-
tionary in letters, the apostle of good taste, could
discern in the creator of " Gargantua " and
" Pantagruel " nothing better than the Rabelais
of legend, the prince of buffoons, the intoxicated
philosopher, who never writ but when he was in
liquor. Swift, on the other hand, was the happy
possessor of all the virtues, in which Rabelais
was lacking—delicacy, choice, taste. So thought
Voltaire, who believed also that " the poetical
numbers of Dean Swift are of a singular and almost
inimitable taste." That is not the opinion of to-day.
The charge commonly brought against his "poetical
numbers " in this later age is that they lack taste
and delicacy, precisely those virtues which Voltaire
gives to them. But nothing changes so rapidly as the
standard of criticism, and Voltaire had not fulfilled
the conditions of understanding, which he had laid
down for others. " Whoever is desirous of understanding Swift," said he, " must visit the island in
which he was born."*

O F *the English poets it was Shakespeare who
influenced Voltaire most profoundly, in Voltaire's
own despite. Shakespeare threw him off his
critical balance, and never did he wholly recover it.
Though he took a certain pride in making Shake-*

The INTRODUCTION.

speare known in France, he was indignant that his countrymen should contemplate the fellow's plays with respect. In his Letter on Tragedy, it is true, he wrote of him with moderation, if not with respect. He admitted that he boasted a strong, fruitful genius, that he was natural and sublime, but he objected on the other side that he had not so much as a single spark of good taste, or knew one word of drama. He called his tragedies monstrous farces, and did not deny that they contained beautiful, noble, dreadful scenes. He was sure that no excuse could be found for the strangling of Desdemona coram populo, and he shuddered at the mere memory of the grave-diggers in Hamlet. Yet when he translated " To be, or not to be," he confessed that his version was but a faint print of a beautiful picture. He never praised him again, and, I think, that the ferocity of his later attacks upon Shakespeare was an act of repentance and regret. He hoped that in the obloquy which he poured upon the head of Shakespeare his more amiable criticism might be forgotten. Henceforth he could not restrain his hand from Shakespeare. In attacking Shakespeare, he believed that he was battling for France, for Corneille, for Racine, for himself. The miscreant, who dared to say a word in praise of Shakespeare was forthwith Voltaire's enemy. When Diderot asserted that Shakespeare was " a Gothic colossus, between whose legs we all could pass," Voltaire accepted the judgment as a personal affront. The translation of Le Tourneur, and its preface, in *which the name of Corneille was not mentioned, was, in Voltaire's eyes, a deliberate attack upon poetry and upon France. He was, he thought and said, fighting for his country. He condescended even to scurrility in his comments upon a poet born two hundred years ago. He called Shakespeare a maniac, a buffoon, a clown. He compared him with Silly Gille of the Fair, " who would express himself with more decency and nobleness than Prince Hamlet." At any defence of Shakespeare, he cried aloud that his country was in danger, and feared that he would " leave France barbarous."**

THE pitched battle was fought on July 26th, 1776, when d'Alembert read before the Academy a piece of writing, which Voltaire had sent from Ferney. It was a very serious performance. Its solemnity ill became what after all was a literary dispute and not a battle to the death of two peoples. Voltaire took his duty and his task with the utmost gravity. " I plead for France," he said. And again : " Shakespeare or Racine must remain in the field." Happily there was and is room in the field for them both. With the death of the relentless Voltaire, a truce was signed, and each of the poets resumed his proper sway. Stendhal presently summed up the case for them both with justice and clarity, and what was once almost a cause of war has become a pleasant topic, which may be discussed across the marble table of a café. It was a favourite subject for the discourse of Verlaine, and none who knew

* See M. J. J. Jusserand's " Shakespeare in France."

that admirable poet and man, Jean Moréas, will forget with what eloquence, at a congenial hour, he would put the two masters each in his place. But it was Voltaire who in his Letters Concerning the English Nation, *first set Shakespeare, with his virtues and his vices, clearly before the critics of France. He had the faculty, which none of his contemporaries shared with him, of attracting a general attention to whatever he wrote or said, and the question—Shakespeare or Racine—which he posed in his* Letters, *a masterpiece of wit, taste and good sense, has been discussed for nearly two hundred years, and has not yet received its final answer.*

CHARLES WHIBLEY.

PUBLISHER'S NOTE: *This edition of* Letters Concerning The English Nation *has been reprinted from the first edition, and is limited to seven hundred and fifty copies for sale.*

THE

PREFACE.

THE present Work appears with Confidence in the Kingdom that gave Birth to it: and will be well satisfied with its Fortune, if it meets with as favourable a Reception as has been indulg'd to all the other Compositions of its Author. The high Esteem which Mr. *de Voltaire* has always discover'd for the *English*, is a Proof how ambitious he is of their Approbation. 'Tis now grown familiar to him, but then he is not tir'd with it; and indeed one wou'd be apt to think that this Circumstance is pleasing to the Nation, from the strong Desire they have to peruse whatever is publish'd under his Name.

WITHOUT pretending therefore to any great Penetration, we may venture to assure him that his Letters will meet with all the Success that cou'd be wish'd. Mr. *de Voltaire* is the Author of them, they were written in *London*, and relate particularly to the *English* Nation; three Circumstances which must necessarily recommend them. The great Freedom

with which Mr. *de Voltaire* delivers himself in his various Observations, cannot
give him any Apprehensions of their
being less favourably receiv'd upon that
Account, by a judicious People who abhor
Flattery. The *English* are pleas'd to have
their Faults pointed out to them, because
this shews at the same Time, that the
Writer is able to distinguish their Merit.

W E must however confess, that these
Letters were not design'd for the Public.
They are the Result of the Author's Com-
placency and Friendship for Mr. *Thiriot*,
who had desir'd him, during his Stay in
England, to favour him with such Re-
marks as he might make on the Manners
and Customs of the *British* Nation. 'Tis
well known that in a Correspondence of
this kind, the most just and regular Writer
does not propose to observe any Method.
Mr. *de Voltaire* in all Probability follow'd
no other Rule in the Choice of his Subjects than his particular Taste, or perhaps
the Queries of his Friend. Be this as it
will, 'twas thought that the most natural
Order in which they cou'd be plac'd,
would be that of their respective Dates.
Several Particulars which are mention'd
in them make it necessary for us to observe, that they were written between the
latter End of 1728, and about 1731. The

only Thing that can be regretted on this Occasion is, that so agreeable a Correspondence should have continued no longer.

THE Reader will no doubt observe, that the Circumstances in every Letter which had not an immediate relation to the Title of it, have been omitted. This was done on purpose; for Letters written with the Confidence and Simplicity of personal Friendship, generally include certain Things which are not proper for the Press. The Public indeed thereby often lose a great many agreeable Particulars; but why should they complain, if the want of them is compensated by a thousand Beauties of another kind? The Variety of the Subjects, the Graces of the Diction, the Solidity of the Reflexions, the delicate Turn of the Criticism; in fine, the noble Fire, which enlivens all the Compositions of Mr. *de Voltaire*, delight the Reader perpetually. Even the most serious Letters, such as those which relate to Sir *Isaac Newton's* Philosophy, will be found entertaining. The Author has infus'd into his Subject all the delicate Touches it was susceptible of; deep and abstruse enough to shew that he was Master of it, and always perspicuous enough to be understood.

S o m e of his *English* Readers may perhaps be dissatisfied at his not expatiating farther on their Constitution and their Laws, which most of them revere almost to Idolatry; but this Reservedness is an Effect of Mr. *de Voltaire's* Judgment. He contented himself with giving his Opinion of them in general Reflexions, the Cast of which is entirely new, and which prove that he had made this Part of the *British* Polity his particular Study. Besides, how was it possible for a Foreigner to pierce thro' their Politicks, that gloomy Labyrinth, in which such of the *English* themselves as are best acquainted with it, confess daily that they are bewilder'd and lost?

THE

CONTENTS.

LETTERS

Concerning the

ENGLISH NATION.

LETTER I.

ON THE

QUAKERS.

I WAS of opinion, that the doctrine and history of so extraordinary a people, were worthy the attention of the curious. To acquaint myself with them, I made a visit to one of the most eminent Quakers in *England*, who after having traded thirty years, had the wisdom to prescribe limits to his fortune and to his desires, and was settled in a little solitude not far from *London*. Being come into it, I perceiv'd a small, but regularly built house, vastly neat, but without the least pomp of furniture.

The Quaker who own'd it, was a hale ruddy complexion'd old man, who had never been afflicted with sickness, because he had always been insensible to passions, and a perfect stranger to intemperance. I never in my life saw a more noble or a more engaging aspect than his. He was dress'd like those of his persuasion, in a plain coat, without pleats in the sides, or buttons on the pockets and sleeves; and had on a beaver, the brims of which were horizontal, like those of our clergy. He did not uncover himself when I appear'd, and advanc'd towards me without once stooping his body; but there appear'd more politeness in the open, humane air of his countenance, than in the custom of drawing one leg behind the other, and taking that from the head, which is made to cover it. Friend, says he to me, I perceive thou art a stranger, but if I can do any thing for thee, only tell me. Sir, says I to him, bending forwards, and advancing as is usual with us, one leg towards him, I flatter myself that my just curiosity will not give you the least offence, and that you'll do me the honour to inform me of the particulars of your religion. The people of thy country, replied the Quaker, are too full of their bows and compliments, but I never yet met with one of them who had so much curiosity as thy self. Come in, and let us first dine together. I still continued to make some very unseasonable ceremonies, it not being easy to disengage one's

self at once from habits we have been long us'd
to; and after taking part of a frugal meal, which
began and ended with a prayer to God, I began
to question my courteous host. I open'd with
that which good Catholicks have more than once
made to Huguenots. My dear sir, says I, were
you ever baptiz'd? I never was, replied the
Quaker, nor any of my brethren. Zounds, says I
to him, you are not Christians then. Friend,
replies the old man in a soft tone of voice, swear
not; we are Christians, and endeavour to be
good Christians, but we are not of opinion, that
the sprinkling water on a child's head makes
him a Christian. Heavens! says I, shock'd at
his impiety, you have then forgot that *Christ*
was baptiz'd by St. *John*. Friend, replies the
mild Quaker once again, swear not. *Christ* indeed was baptiz'd by *John*, but he himself never
baptiz'd any one. We are the disciples of *Christ*,
not of *John*. I pitied very much the sincerity of
my worthy Quaker, and was absolutely for forcing him to get himself christned. Were that all,
replied he very gravely, we would submit chear-
fully to baptism, purely in compliance with thy
weakness, for we don't condemn any person
who uses it; but then we think, that those who
profess a religion of so holy, so spiritual a nature
as that of *Christ*, ought to abstain to the utmost
of their power from the *Jewish* ceremonies. O
unaccountable! says I, what! baptism a *Jewish*
ceremony? Yes, my friend says he, so truly

Jewish, that a great many *Jews* use the baptism of *John* to this day. Look into ancient authors, and thou wilt find that *John* only reviv'd this practice; and that it had been us'd by the *Hebrews*, long before his time, in like manner as the Mahometans imitated the *Ishmaelites* in their pilgrimages to *Mecca*. *Jesus* indeed submitted to the baptism of *John*, as he had suffer'd himself to be circumcis'd; but circumcision and the washing with water ought to be abolish'd by the baptism of *Christ*, that baptism of the spirit, that ablution of the soul, which is the salvation of mankind. Thus the forerunner said, *I indeed baptize you with water unto repentance; but he that cometh after me, is mightier than I, whose shoes I am not worthy to bear: he shall baptize you with the Holy Ghost and with fire.* Likewise *Paul* the great apostle of the Gentiles, writes as follows to the *Corinthians; Christ sent me not to baptize, but to preach the Gospel;†* and indeed *Paul* never baptiz'd but two persons with water, and that very much against his inclinations. He circumcis'd his disciple *Timothy*, and the other disciples likewise circumcis'd all who were willing to submit to that carnal ordinance. But art thou circumcis'd, added he? I have not the honour to be so, says I. Well, friend, continues the Quaker, thou art a Christian without being circumcis'd, and I am one without being baptiz'd. Thus did this pious

* St. Matth. iii, 11.   † I Cor. i, 17.

man make a wrong, but very specious application, of four or five texts of scripture which seem'd to favour the tenets of his sect; but at the same time forgot very sincerely an hundred texts which made directly against them. I had more sense than to contest with him, since there is no possibility of convincing an enthusiast. A man shou'd never pretend to inform a lover of his mistress's faults, no more than one who is at law, of the badness of his cause; nor attempt to win over a fanatic by strength of reasoning. Accordingly I wav'd the subject.

WELL, says I to him, what sort of a communion have you? We have none like that thou hintest at among us, replied he. How! no communion, says I? Only that spiritual one, replied he, of hearts. He then began again to throw out his texts of scripture; and preach'd a most eloquent sermon against that ordinance. He harangued in a tone as tho' he had been inspir'd, to prove that the sacraments were merely of human invention, and that the word *sacrament*, was not once mention'd in the gospel. Excuse, says he, my ignorance, for I have not employ'd an hundredth part of the arguments which might be brought, to prove the truth of our religion, but these thou thy self mayest peruse in the Exposition of our Faith written by *Robert Barclay*. 'Tis one of the best pieces that ever was penn'd by man; and as our adversaries confess it to be of dangerous tendency, the argu-

ments in it must necessarily be very convincing.
I promis'd to peruse this piece, and my Quaker
imagin'd he had already made a convert of me.
He afterwards gave me an account in few words,
of some singularities which make this sect the
contempt of others. Confess, says he, that 'twas
very difficult for thee to refrain from laughter,
when I answer'd all thy civilities without un-
covering my head, and at the same time said
Thee and *Thou* to thee. However, thou appearest
to me too well read, not to know that in *Christ's*
time no nation was so ridiculous as to put the
plural number for the singular. *Augustus Cæsar*
himself was spoke to in such phrases as these, *I
love thee, I beseech thee, I thank thee;* but he did
not allow any person to call him *Domine,* Sir.
'Twas not till many ages after, that men wou'd
have the word *You,* as tho' they were double,
instead of *Thou* employ'd in speaking to them;
and usurp'd the flattering titles of lordship, of
eminence, and of holiness, which mere worms
bestow on other worms, by assuring them that
they are with a most profound respect, and an
infamous falshood, their most obedient, humble
servants. 'Tis to secure our selves more strongly
from such a shameless traffick of lies and flattery,
that we *thee* and *thou* a king with the same freedom as we do a beggar, and salute no person;
we owing nothing to mankind but charity, and
to the laws respect and obedience.

O U R apparel is also somewhat different from

that of others, and this purely, that it may be a
perpetual warning to us not to imitate them.
Others wear the badges and marks of their several
dignities, and we those of christian humility.
We fly from all assemblies of pleasure, from
diversions of every kind, and from places where
gaming is practis'd; and indeed our case wou'd
be very deplorable, should we fill with such
levities as those I have mention'd, the heart
which ought to be the habitation of God. We
never swear, not even in a court of justice, being
of opinion that the most holy name of God
ought not to be prostituted in the miserable
contests betwixt man and man. When we are
oblig'd to appear before a magistrate upon other
people's account (for law-suits are unknown
among the friends) we give evidence to the truth
by sealing it with our *yea* or *nay*; and the judges
believe us on our bare affirmation, whilst so
many other Christians forswear themselves on
the holy Gospels. We never war or fight in any
case; but 'tis not that we are afraid, for so far
from shuddering at the thoughts of death, we
on the contrary bless the moment which unites
us with the Being of Beings; but the reason of
our not using the outward sword is, that we are
neither wolves, tygers, nor mastiffs, but men
and Christians. Our God, who has commanded
us to love our enemies, and to suffer without
repining, would certainly not permit us to cross
the seas, merely because murtherers cloath'd in

scarlet, and wearing caps two foot high enlist
citizens by a noise made with two little sticks
on an ass's skin extended. And when, after a
victory is gain'd, the whole city of *London* is
illuminated; when the sky is in a blaze with fire-
works, and a noise is heard in the air of thanks-
givings, of bells, of organs, and of the cannon,
we groan in silence, and are deeply affected
with sadness of spirit and brokenness of heart,
for the sad havock which is the occasion of those
public rejoycings.

LETTER II.

ON THE

QUAKERS.

SUCH was the substance of the conversation I had with this very singular person; but I was greatly surpriz'd to see him come the *Sunday* following, and take me with him to the Quaker's meeting. There are several of these in *London*, but that which he carried me to stands near the famous pillar call'd the monument. The brethren were already assembled at my entring it with my guide. There might be about four hundred men and three hundred women in the meeting. The women hid their faces behind their fans, and the men were cover'd with their broad-brimm'd hats; all were seated, and the silence was universal. I past through them, but did not perceive so much as one lift up his eyes to look at me. This silence lasted a quarter of an hour, when at last one of them rose up, took off his hat, and after making a variety of wry faces, and groaning in a most lamentable manner, he partly from his nose, and partly from his mouth, threw out a strange, confus'd jumble of words, (borrow'd as he imagin'd from the Gospel) which neither himself nor any of his hearers understood. When this distorter had ended his beautiful soliloquy, and that the stupid, but greatly edified, congregation were separated, I ask'd my friend how it was possible for the judicious part of their assembly to suffer such a babbling. We are oblig'd, says he, to suffer it, because no one knows when a man rises up to hold forth, whether he will be mov'd by the spirit or by folly. In this doubt and uncertainty we listen patiently to every one, we even allow our women to hold forth; two or three of these are often inspir'd at one and the same time, and 'tis then that a most charming noise is heard in the Lord's house. You have then no priests, says I to him. No, no, friend, replies the Quaker, to our great happiness. Then opening one of the friend's books, as he call'd it, he read the following words: in an emphatic tone: God forbid we should presume to ordain any one to receive the holy spirit on the Lord's day, to the prejudice of the rest of the brethren. Thanks to the almighty, we are the only people upon earth that have no priests. Wouldest thou deprive us of so happy a distinction? Why shou'd we abandon our babe to mercenary nurses, when we our selves have milk enough for it? These mercenary creatures

wou'd soon domineer in our houses, and destroy
both the mother and the babe. God has said,
freely you have receiv'd, freely give. Shall we
after these words cheapen, as it were, the Gospel;
sell the Holy Ghost, and make of an assembly
of Christians a mere shop of traders. We don't
pay a sett of men cloath'd in black, to assist our
poor, to bury our dead, or to preach to the
brethren; these offices are all of too tender a
nature, for us ever to entrust them to others.
But how is it possible for you, says I, with some
warmth, to know whether your discourse is
really inspir'd by the Almighty? Whosoever,
says he, shall implore *Christ* to enlighten him,
and shall publish the Gospel truths he may
feel inwardly, such an one may be assur'd that
he is inspir'd by the Lord. He then pour'd forth
a numberless multitude of Scripture-texts, which
prov'd, as he imagin'd, that there is no such
thing as Christianity without an immediate revelation, and added these remarkable words:
When thou movest one of thy limbs, is it mov'd
by thy own power? Certainly not, for this limb
is often sensible to involuntary motions; consequently he who created thy body, gives motion
to this earthly tabernacle. And are the several
ideas of which thy soul receives the impression
form'd by thy self? Much less are they, since
these pour in upon thy mind whether thou wilt
or no; consequently thou receivest thy ideas
from him who created thy soul: But as he leaves

thy affections at full liberty, he gives thy mind such ideas as thy affections may deserve; if thou livest in God, thou actest, thou thinkest in God. After this thou needest only but open thine eyes to that light which enlightens all mankind, and 'tis then thou wilt perceive the truth, and make others perceive it. Why this, says I, is *Malbranche's* doctrine to a tittle. I am acquainted with thy *Malbranche*, says he; he had something of the *friend* in him, but was not enough so. These are the most considerable particulars I learnt concerning the doctrine of the Quakers; in my next letter I shall acquaint you with their history, which you will find more singular than their opinions.

L E T T E R III.

O N T H E

Q U A K E R S.

YOU have already heard that the Quakers date from *Christ*, who according to them was the first Quaker. Religion, say these, was corrupted, a little after his death, and remain'd in that state of corruption about 1600 Years. But there were always a few Quakers conceal'd in the world, who carefully preserv'd the sacred fire, which was extinguish'd in all but themselves, 'till at last this light spread it self in *England* in 1642.

'T W A S at the time when *Great Britain* was torn to pieces by the intestine wars, which three or four sects had rais'd in the name of God, that one *George Fox*, born in *Leicestershire*, and son to a silk-weaver, took it into his head to preach; and, as he pretended, with all the requisites of a true apostle, that is, without being able either to read or write. He was about twenty five* years

* *Fox* could read at that age.

of age, irreproachable in his life and conduct, and a holy mad-man. He was equip'd in leather from head to foot, and travell'd from one village to another, exclaiming against war and the clergy. Had his invectives been levell'd against the soldiery only, he wou'd have been safe enough, but he inveigh'd against ecclesiasticks. *Fox* was seiz'd at *Derby*, and being carried before a justice of peace; he did not once offer to pull off his leathern hat; upon which an officer gave him a great box o'th' ear, and cried to him, Don't you know you are to appear uncover'd before his worship? *Fox* presented his other cheek to the officer, and begg'd him to give him another box for God's sake. The justice wou'd have had him sworn before he ask'd him any questions: Know, friend, says *Fox* to him, that I never swear. The justice observing he *Thee'd* and *Thou'd* him, sent him to the house of correction in *Derby*, with orders that he should be whipp'd there. *Fox* prais'd the Lord all the way he went to the house of correction, where the justice's order was executed with the utmost severity. The men who whipp'd this enthusiast, were greatly surpriz'd to hear him beseech them to give him a few more lashes for the good of his soul. There was no need of intreating these people; the lashes were repeated, for which *Fox* thank'd them very cordially, and began to preach. At first, the spectators fell a laughing, but they afterwards listned to him; and as enthusiasm is an epidemical distemper, many were persuaded, and those who scourg'd him became his first disciples. Being set at liberty, he ran up and down the country with a dozen proselytes at his heels, still declaiming against the clergy, and was whipp'd from time to time. Being one day set in the pillory, he harangued the crowd in so strong and moving a manner, that fifty of the auditors became his converts; and he won the rest so much in his favour, that his head being freed tumultuously from the hole where it was fastned, the populace went and search'd for the church of *England* clergyman, who had been chiefly instrumental in bringing him to this punishment, and set him on the same pillory where *Fox* had stood.

F o x was bold enough to convert some of *Oliver Cromwell's* Soldiers, who thereupon quitted the service and refus'd to take the oaths. *Oliver* having as great a contempt for a sect which would not allow its members to fight, as *Sixtus Quintus* had for another sect, *Dove non si chiavava*, began to persecute these new converts. The prisons were crouded with them, but persecution seldom has any other effect than to increase the number of proselytes. These came therefore from their confinement, more strongly confirmed in the principles they had imbib'd, and follow'd by their gaolers whom they had brought over to their belief. But the circumstances which contributed chiefly to the spreading of this sect were as follows. *Fox* thought himself inspir'd, and consequently was of opinion, that he must speak in a manner different from the rest of mankind. He thereupon began to writhe his body, to screw up his face, to hold in his breath, and to exhale it in a forcible manner, insomuch that the priestess of the *Pythian* God at *Delphos* could not have acted her part to better advantage. Inspiration soon became so habitual to him, that he cou'd scarce deliver himself in any other manner. This was the first gift he communicated to his disciples. These ap'd very sincerely their master's several grimaces, and shook in every limb the instant the fit of inspiration came upon them, whence they were call'd Quakers. The vulgar attempted to mimick them, they trembled, they spake thro' the nose; they quak'd and fancied themselves inspir'd by the Holy Ghost. The only thing now wanting was a few miracles, and accordingly they wrought some.

FOX, this modern patriarch, spoke thus to a justice of peace, before a large assembly of people. Friend, take care what thou dost: God will soon punish thee for persecuting his saints. This magistrate being one who besotted himself every day with bad beer and brandy, died of an apoplexy two days after, the moment he had sign'd a *mittimus* for imprisoning some Quakers. The sudden death with which this justice was seiz'd, was not ascrib'd to his intemperance, but was universally look'd upon as the effect of the holy man's predictions; so that this accident made more converts to Quakerism, than a thousand sermons and as many shaking fits cou'd have done. *Oliver* finding them increase daily was desirous of bringing them over to his party, and for that purpose attempted to bribe them by money. However, they were incorruptible, which made him one day declare, that this religion was the only one he had ever met with that had resisted the charms of gold.

T H E Quakers were several times persecuted under *Charles* the second, not upon a religious account, but for refusing to pay the tythes, for *Thee-ing* and *Thou-ing* the magistrates, and for refusing to take the oaths enacted by the laws.

A T last *Robert Barclay*, a native of *Scotland*, presented to the king in 1675, his apology for the Quakers, a work as well drawn up as the subject cou'd possibly admit. The dedication to *Charles* the second is not fill'd with mean, flattering encomiums; but abounds with bold touches in favour of truth, and with the wisest counsels. " Thou hast tasted," says he to the king at the close of his epistle dedicatory, " of " prosperity and adversity; thou knowest what " it is to be banished thy native country; to be " over-rul'd as well as to rule, and sit upon the " throne; and being oppressed, thou hast reason " to know how hateful the oppressor is both to " God and man: If after all these warnings and

" advertisements, thou dost not turn unto the
" Lord with all thy heart; but forget him who
" remembered thee in thy distress, and give up
" thy self to follow lust and vanity, surely great
" will be thy condemnation.

" AGAINST which snare, as well as the
" temptation of those, that may or do feed thee,
" and prompt thee to evil, the most excellent
" and prevalent remedy will be, to apply thy
" self to that light of *Christ*, which shineth in
" thy conscience, which neither can nor will
" flatter thee, nor suffer thee to be at ease in thy
" sins; but doth and will deal plainly and faith-
" fully with thee, as those, that are followers
" thereof have plainly done —— *Thy faithful*
" *friend and subject*, ROBERT BARCLAY.

A more surprizing circumstance is, that this
epistle, written by a private man of no figure,
was so happy in its effects as to put a stop to the
persecution.

LETTER IV.

ON THE

QUAKERS.

ABOUT this * time arose the illustrious *William Pen,* who establish'd the power of the Quakers in *America,* and would have made them appear venerable in the eyes of the *Europeans,* were it possible for mankind to respect virtue, when reveal'd in a ridiculous light. He was the only son of vice-admiral *Pen,* favourite to the duke of *York,* afterwards king *James* the second.

WILLIAM PEN at twenty years of age happening to meet with a † Quaker in *Cork,* whom he had known at *Oxford,* this man made a proselyte of him; and *William* being a sprightly youth, and naturally eloquent, having a winning aspect, and a very engaging carriage, he soon gain'd over some of his Intimates. He carried matters so far that he form'd by insensible degrees a society of young Quakers who met at his

* 1666.   † *Thomas Loe.*

house; so that he was at the head of a sect when a little above twenty.

B E I N G return'd, after his leaving *Cork*, to the vice-admiral his father, instead of falling upon his knees to ask him blessing, he went up to him with his hat on, and said, Friend, I'm very glad to see thee in good health. The vice-admiral imagin'd his son to be crazy; but soon finding he was turn'd Quaker, he employ'd all the methods that prudence could suggest, to engage him to behave and act like other people. The youth made no other answer to his father, than by exhorting him to turn Quaker also. At last his father confin'd himself to this single request, *viz.* that he shou'd wait upon the king and the duke of *York* with his hat under his arm, and shou'd not *Thee* and *Thou* them. *William* answer'd, that he could not do these things for conscience sake, which exasperated his father to such a degree, that he turn'd him out of doors. Young *Pen* gave God thanks, for permitting him to suffer so early in his cause, after which he went into the city, where he held forth,* and made a great number of converts.

T H E church of *England* clergy found their congregations dwindle away daily; and *Pen* being young, handsome, and of a graceful stature, the court as well as the city ladies flock'd very devoutly to his meeting. The patriarch *George Fox* hearing of his great reputation, came

* About 1668, and the 24th year of his age.

to *London*, (tho' the journey was very long) purely to see and converse with him. Both resolv'd to go upon missions into foreign countries, and accordingly they embark'd for *Holland*, after having left labourers sufficient to take care of the *London* vineyard.

THEIR labours were crown'd with success in *Amsterdam;* but a circumstance which reflected the greatest honour on them, and at the same time put their humility to the greatest trial, was the reception they met with from *Elizabeth* the princess of *Palatine*, aunt to *George* the first of *Great-Britain*, a lady conspicuous for her genius and knowledge, and to whom *Des Cartes* had dedicated his *Philosophical Romance*.

SHE was then retir'd to the *Hague*, where she receiv'd these *friends*, for so the Quakers were at that time call'd in *Holland*. This princess had several conferences with them in her palace, and she at last entertain'd so favourable an opinion of Quakerism, that they confess'd she was not far from the kingdom of heaven. The friends sow'd likewise the good seed in *Germany*, but reap'd very little fruit; for the mode of *Thee-ing* and *Thou-ing* was not approv'd of in a country, where a man is perpetually oblig'd to employ the titles of highness and excellency. *William Pen* return'd soon to *England* upon hearing of his father's sickness, in order to see him before he died. The vice-admiral was reconcil'd to his son, and tho' of a different persuasion, embrac'd him tenderly. *William* made a fruitless exhortation to his father not to receive the sacrament, but to die a Quaker; and the good old man intreated his son *William* to wear buttons on his sleeves, and a crape hatband in his beaver, but all to no purpose.

W I L L I A M   P E N inherited very large possessions, part of which consisted in crown-debts due to the vice-admiral for sums he had advanc'd for the sea-service. No monies were at that time more secure than those owing from the king. *Pen* was oblig'd to go more than once, and *Thee* and *Thou* king *Charles* and his ministers, in order to recover the debt; and at last instead of specie, the government invested him with the right and sovereignty of a province of *America*, to the south of *Maryland*. Thus was a Quaker rais'd to sovereign power. *Pen* set sail for his new dominions with two ships freighted with Quakers, who follow'd his fortune. The country was then call'd *Pensilvania* from *William Pen*, who there founded *Philadelphia*, now the most flourishing city in that country. The first step he took was to enter into an alliance with his *American* neighbours; and this is the only treaty between those people and the Christians that was not ratified by an oath, and was never infring'd. The new sovereign was at the same time the legislator of *Pensilvania*, and enacted very wise and prudent laws, none of which have ever been chang'd since his time. The first is, to injure no person upon a religious account, and to consider as brethren all those who believe in one God.

HE had no sooner settled his government, but several *American* merchants came and peopled this colony. The natives of the country instead of flying into the woods, cultivated by insensible degrees a friendship with the peaceable Quakers. They lov'd these foreigners as much as they detested the other Christians who had conquer'd and laid waste *America*. In a little time, a great number of these savages (falsely so call'd) charm'd with the mild and gentle disposition of their neighbours, came in crowds to *William Pen*, and besought him to admit them into the number of his vassals. 'Twas very rare and uncommon for a sovereign to be *Thee'd* and *Thou'd* by the meanest of his subjects, who never took their hats off when they come into his presence; and as singular for a government to be without one priest in it, and for a people to be without arms, either offensive or defensive; for a body of citizens to be absolutely undistinguish'd but by the publick employments, and for neighbours not to entertain the least jealousy one against the other.

WILLIAM PEN might glory in having brought down upon earth the so much boasted golden age, which in all probability never existed but in *Pensilvania*. He return'd to *England* to settle some affairs relating to his new dominions. After the death of king *Charles* the second,

king *James*, who had lov'd the father, indulg'd
the same affection to the son, and no longer
consider'd him as an obscure Sectary, but as a
very great man. The king's politicks on this
occasion agreed with his inclinations. He was
desirous of pleasing the Quakers, by annulling
the laws made against Nonconformists, in order
to have an opportunity, by this universal toleration, of establishing the *Romish* religion. All the
sectarists in *England* saw the snare that was laid
for them, but did not give into it; they never
failing to unite when the *Romish* religion, their
common enemy, is to be oppos'd. But *Pen* did
not think himself bound in any manner to re-
nounce his principles, merely to favour Protes-
tants to whom he was odious, in opposition to a
king who lov'd him. He had establish'd an universal toleration with regard to conscience in
America, and wou'd not have it thought that he
intended to destroy it in *Europe;* for which
reason he adhered so inviolably to king *James*,
that a report prevail'd universally of his being
a Jesuit. This calumny affected him very
strongly and he was oblig'd to justify himself
in print. However, the unfortunate king *James*
the second, in whom, as in most princes of the
Stuart family, grandeur and weakness were
equally blended; and who, like them, as much
overdid some things as he was short in others,
lost his kingdom in a manner that is hardly to
be accounted for.

ALL the *English* sectarists accepted from *William* the third and his parliament, the toleration and indulgence which they had refus'd when offer'd by king *James*. 'Twas then the Quakers began to enjoy, by virtue of the laws, the several privileges they possess at this time. *Pen* having at last seen Quakerism firmly establish'd in his native country, went back to *Pensilvania*. His own people and the *Americans* receiv'd him with tears of joy, as tho' he had been a father who was return'd to visit his children. All the laws had been religiously observ'd in his absence, a circumstance in which no legislator had ever been happy but himself. After having resided some years in *Pensilvania*, he left it, but with great reluctance, in order to return to *England*, there to solicit some matters in favour of the commerce of *Pensilvania*. But he never saw it again, he dying in *Ruscomb* in *Berkshire*, *anno* 1718.

I AM not able to guess what fate Quakerism may have in *America*, but I perceive it dwindles away daily in *England*. In all countries where liberty of conscience is allow'd, the establish'd religion will at last swallow up all the rest. Quakers are disqualified from being members of parliament; nor can they enjoy any post or preferment, because an oath must always be taken on these occasions, and they never swear. They are therefore reduc'd to the necessity of subsisting upon traffick. Their children, whom the industry of their parents has enrich'd, are desirous of enjoying honours, of wearing buttons and ruffles; and quite asham'd of being call'd Quakers, they become converts to the Church of *England*, merely to be in the fashion.

LETTER V.

ON THE

CHURCH

OF

ENGLAND.

ENGLAND is properly the country of sectarists. *Multæ sunt mansiones in domo patris mei* (in my father's house are many mansions.) An *Englishman*, as one to whom liberty is natural, may go to heaven his own way.

NEVERTHELESS, tho' every one is permitted to serve God in whatever mode of fashion he thinks proper, yet their true religion, that in which a man makes his fortune, is the sect of Episcoparians or Churchmen, call'd the Church of *England*, or simply the Church, by way of eminence. No person can possess an employment either in *England* or *Ireland*, unless he be

rank'd among the faithful, that is, professes
himself a member of the Church of *England*.
This reason (which carries mathematical evidence with it) has converted such numbers of
dissenters of all persuasions, that not a twentieth
part of the nation is out of the pale of the establish'd church. The *English* clergy have retain'd
a great number of the Romish ceremonies, and
especially that of receiving, with a most scrupulous attention, their tithes. They also have the
pious ambition to aim at superiority.

MOREOVER, they inspire very religiously
their flock with a holy zeal against Dissenters
of all denominations. This zeal was pretty violent
under the Tories, in the four last years of queen
Anne; but was productive of no greater mischief
than the breaking the windows of some meeting-
houses, and the demolishing of a few of them.
For religious rage ceas'd in *England* with the
civil wars; and was no more under queen *Anne*,
than the hollow noise of a sea whose billows
still heav'd, tho' so long after the storm, when
the Whigs and Tories laid waste their native
country, in the same manner as the Guelphs
and Gibelins formerly did theirs. 'Twas absolutely necessary for both parties to call in religion on this occasion; the Tories declar'd for
episcopacy, and the Whigs, as some imagin'd,
were for abolishing it; however, after these had
got the upper hand, they contented themselves
with only abridging its power.

A T the time when the earl of *Oxford* and the lord *Bolingbroke* us'd to drink healths to the Tories, the Church of *England* consider'd those noblemen as the defenders of it's holy privileges. The lower house of Convocation (a kind of house of Commons) compos'd wholly of the clergy, was in some credit at that time; at least the members of it had the liberty to meet, to dispute on ecclesiastical matters, to sentence impious books from time to time to the flames, that is, books written against themselves. The ministry, which is now compos'd of Whigs, does not so much as allow those gentlemen to assemble, so that they are at this time reduc'd (in the obscurity of their respective parishes) to the melancholy occupation of praying for the prosperity of the government, whose tranquillity they would willingly disturb. With regard to the bishops, who are twenty six in all, they still have seats in the house of lords in spite of the Whigs, because the ancient abuse of consider-ing them as Barons subsists to this day. There is a clause however in the oath which the gov-ernment requires from these gentlemen, that puts their christian patience to a very great trial, *viz.* that they shall be of the Church of *England* as by law establish'd. There are few bishops, deans, or other dignitaries, but imagine they are so *jure divino ;* 'tis consequently a great morti-fication to them to be oblig'd to confess, that they owe their dignity to a pitiful law enacted

by a sett of profane laymen. A learned monk
(father *Courayer*) writ a book lately to prove the
validity and succession of *English* ordinations.
This book was forbid in *France;* but do you
believe that the *English* ministry were pleas'd
with it? Far from it. Those damn'd Whigs don't
value a straw, whether the episcopal succession
among them hath been interrupted or not, or
whether bishop *Parker* was consecrated (as 'tis
pretended) in a tavern, or a church; for these
Whigs are much better pleas'd that the bishops
should derive their authority from the parliament, than from the apostles. The lord *B*——
observ'd, that this notion of divine right would
only make so many tyrants in lawn-sleeves, but
that the laws made so many citizens.

W I T H regard to the morals of the *English*
clergy, they are more regular than those of
France, and for this reason. All the clergy (a
very few excepted) are educated in the universities of *Oxford* or *Cambridge*, far from the de-
pravity and corruption which reign in the capital.
They are not call'd to dignities till very late, in
an Age when men are sensible of no other passion
but avarice, that is, when their ambition craves
a supply. Employments are here bestow'd both
in the church and the army, as a reward for long
services; and we never see youngsters made
bishops or colonels immediately upon their
laying aside the academical gown; and besides,
most of the clergy are married. The stiff and

awkward air contracted by them at the university, and the little familiarity the men of this
country have with the ladies, commonly oblige
a bishop to confine himself to, and rest contented with his own. Clergymen sometimes take
a glass at the tavern, custom giving them a sanction on this occasion; and if they fuddle themselves 'tis in a very serious manner, and without
giving the least scandal.

THAT sable mix'd being (not to be defin'd)
who is neither of the clergy nor of the laity; in
a word, the thing call'd *Abbé* in *France*, is a
species quite unknown in *England*. All the clergy
here are very much upon the reserve, and most
of them pedants. When these are told, that in
France, young fellows famous for their dissolute-
ness and rais'd to the highest dignities of the
church by female intrigues, address the fair
publickly in an amorous way, amuse themselves
in writing tender love-songs, entertain their
friends very splendidly every night at their own
houses, and after the banquet is ended, with-
draw to invoke the assistance of the Holy Ghost,
and call themselves boldly the successors of the
apostles, they bless God for their being Protes-
tants. But, these are shameless Hereticks, who
deserve to be blown hence thro' the flames to
old Nick, as *Rabelais* says, and for this reason I
don't trouble my self about them.

LETTER VI.

ON THE

PRESBYTERIANS.

THE Church of *England* is confin'd almost to the kingdom whence it receiv'd its name, and to *Ireland*, for Presbyterianism is the establish'd religion in *Scotland*. This Presbyterianism is directly the same with Calvinism, as it was establish'd in *France*, and is now profess'd at *Geneva*. As the priests of this sect receive but very inconsiderable stipends from their churches, and consequently cannot emulate the splendid luxury of bishops, they exclaim very naturally against honours which they can never attain to. Figure to yourself the haughty *Diogenes*, trampling under foot the pride of *Plato*. The *Scotch* Presbyterians are not very unlike that proud, tho' tatter'd reasoner. *Diogenes* did not use *Alexander* half so impertinently as these treated king *Charles* the second; for when they took up arms in his cause, in opposition to *Oliver*, who had deceiv'd them, they forc'd that poor monarch to undergo the hearing of three or four sermons every day; wou'd not suffer him to play, reduc'd him to a state of penitence and mortification; so that *Charles* soon grew sick of these pedants, and accordingly elop'd from them with as much joy as a youth does from school.

A Church of *England* minister appears as another *Cato* in presence of a juvenile, sprightly *French* graduate, who bawls for a whole morning together in the divinity schools, and hums a song in chorus with ladies in the evening: But this *Cato* is a very spark, when before a *Scotch* Presbyterian. The latter affects a serious gate, puts on a sour look, wears a vastly broad-brimm'd hat, and a long cloak over a very short coat; preaches thro' the nose, and gives the name of the whore of *Babylon* to all churches, where the ministers are so fortunate as to enjoy an annual revenue of five or six thousand pounds; and where the people are weak enough to suffer this, and to give them the titles of my lord, your lordship, or your eminence.

T H E S E gentlemen, who have also some churches in *England*, introduc'd there the mode of grave and severe exhortations. To them is owing the sanctification of *Sunday* in the three kingdoms. People are there forbid to work or take any recreation on that day, in which the severity is twice as great as that of the *Romish* church. No opera's, plays or concerts are

D

allow'd in *London* on *Sundays;* and even cards
are so expressly forbid, that none but persons of
quality and those we call the genteel, play on that
day; the rest of the nation go either to church,
to the tavern, or to see their mistresses.

THO' the Episcopal and Presbyterian sects
are the two prevailing ones in *Great-Britain*,
yet all others are very welcome to come and
settle in it, and live very sociably together, tho'
most of their preachers hate one another almost
as cordially as a Jansenist damns a Jesuit.

TAKE a view of the *Royal-Exchange* in
London, a place more venerable than many
courts of justice, where the representatives of
all nations meet for the benefit of mankind.
There the Jew, the Mahometan, and the Christian transact together as tho' they all profess'd
the same religion, and give the name of Infidel
to none but bankrupts. There the Presbyterian
confides in the Anabaptist, and the Churchman
depends on the Quaker's word. At the breaking
up of this pacific and free assembly, some with-
draw to the synagogue, and others to take a
glass. This man goes and is baptiz'd in a
great tub, in the name of the Father, Son, and
Holy Ghost: That man has his son's foreskin
cut off, whilst a sett of *Hebrew* words (quite unintelligible to him) are mumbled over his child.
Others retire to their churches, and there wait
for the inspiration of heaven with their hats on,
and all are satisfied.

I F one religion only were allowed in *England*, the government would very possibly become arbitrary; if there were but two, the people wou'd cut one another's throats; but as there are such a multitude, they all live happy and in peace.

LETTER VII.

ON THE

SOCINIANS,

OR

ARIANS,

OR

ANTITRINITARIANS.

THERE is a little sect here compos'd of clergymen, and of a few very learned persons among the laity, who, tho' they don't call themselves *Arians* or *Socinians*, do yet dissent entirely from St. *Athanasius*, with regard to their notions of the Trinity, and declare very frankly, that the Father is greater than the Son.

D o you remember what is related of a certain

orthodox bishop, who in order to convince an
emperor of the reality of consubstantiation,
put his hand under the chin of the monarch's
son, and took him by the nose in presence of
his sacred majesty? The emperor was going to
order his attendants to throw the bishop out of
the window, when the good old man gave him
this convincing reason: Since your majesty,
says he, is angry when your son has not due respect shown him, what punishment do you
think will God the father inflict on those who
refuse his son *Jesus* the titles due to him? The
persons I just now mention'd, declare that the
holy bishop took a very strong step; that his
argument was inconclusive, and that the emperor should have answer'd him thus: Know
that there are two ways by which men may be
wanting in respect to me; first, in not doing
honour sufficient to my son; and secondly, in
paying him the same honour as to me.

B E this as it will, the principles of *Arius* began to revive, not only in *England* but in *Holland*
and *Poland*. The celebrated sir *Isaac Newton*
honour'd this opinion so far as to countenance
it. This philosopher thought that the Unitarians
argued more mathematically than we do. But
the most sanguine stickler for Arianism is the
illustrious Dr. *Clark*. This man is rigidly
virtuous, and of a mild disposition; is more
fond of his tenets than desirous of propagating
them; and absorb'd so entirely in problems

and calculations, that he is a mere reasoning
machine.

'T I S he who wrote a book which is much
esteem'd and little understood, on the existence
of God; and another more intelligible, but
pretty much contemned, on the truth of the
Christian religion.

H E never engag'd in scholastic disputes,
which our friend calls venerable trifles. He only
publish'd a work containing all the testimonies
of the primitive ages, for and against the Unitarians, and leaves to the reader the counting
of the voices, and the liberty of forming a judgment. This book won the doctor a great number
of partizans, and lost him the See of *Canterbury*:
But in my humble opinion, he was out in his
calculation, and had better have been Primate
of all *England*, than meerly an *Arian* parson.

Y O U see that opinions are subject to revolutions as well as Empires. *Arianism* after having
triumph'd during three centuries, and then
forgot twelve, rises at last out of its own ashes;
but it has chose a very improper season to make
its appearance in, the present age being quite
cloy'd with disputes and Sects. The members
of this Sect are, besides, too few to be indulg'd
the liberty of holding public assemblies, which
however they will doubtless be permitted to do,
in case they spread considerably. But people
are now so very cold with respect to all things
of this kind, that there is little probability any

new religion, or old one that may be reviv'd, will meet with favour. Is it not whimsical enough that *Luther*, *Calvin* and *Zuinglius*, all of 'em wretched authors, should have founded Sects which are now spread over a great part of *Europe;* that *Mahomet*, tho' so ignorant, should have given a religion to *Asia* and *Africa;* and that Sir *Isaac Newton*, Dr. *Clark*, Mr. *Locke*, Mr. *Le Clerc &c.* the greatest philosophers, as well as the ablest writers of their ages, should scarce have been able to raise a little flock, which even decreases daily.

THIS it is to be born at a proper period of time. Were Cardinal *de Retz* to return again into the world, neither his eloquence nor his intrigues would draw together ten women in *Paris*.

WERE *Oliver Cromwell*, he who beheaded his Sovereign and seiz'd upon the kingly dignity, to rise from the dead, he wou'd be a wealthy city trader, and no more.

LETTER VIII.

ON THE

PARLIAMENT.

THE Members of the *English* Parliament are fond of comparing themselves to the old *Romans*.

NOT long since, Mr. *Shippen* open'd a speech in the house of Commons with these words, *The Majesty of the People of* England *would be wounded*. The singularity of the expression occasion'd a loud laugh; but this Gentleman, so far from being disconcerted, repeated the same words with a resolute tone of voice, and the laugh ceas'd. In my opinion, the Majesty of the people of *England* has nothing in common with that of the people of *Rome*, much less is there any affinity between their governments. There is in *London* a Senate, some of the members whereof are accus'd, (doubtless very unjustly) of selling their voices on certain occasions, as was done in *Rome ;* this is the only resemblance. Besides, the two nations appear to me quite opposite in character, with regard both to good and evil. The *Romans* never knew the dreadful folly of religious Wars, an abomination reserv'd for devout Preachers of patience and humility. *Marius* and *Sylla*, *Cæsar* and *Pompey*, *Anthony* and *Augustus*, did not draw their swords and set the world in a blaze, merely to determine whether the *Flamen* should wear his shirt over his robe, or his robe over his shirt; or whether the sacred Chickens should eat and drink, or eat only, in order to take the augury. The *English* have hang'd one another by law, and cut one another to pieces in pitch battles, for quarrels of as trifling a nature. The Sects of the Episcoparians and Presbyterians quite distracted these very serious Heads for a time. But I fancy they'll hardly ever be so silly again, they seeming to be grown wiser at their own expence; and I don't perceive the least inclination in them to murther one another merely about syllogisms, as some Zealots among them once did.

B U T here follows a more essential difference between *Rome* and *England*, which gives the advantage entirely to the latter, *viz.* that the civil wars of *Rome* ended in slavery, and those of the *English* in liberty. The *English* are the only people upon earth who have been able to prescribe limits to the power of Kings by resisting them; and who, by a series of struggles, have at last establish'd that wise Government, where the Prince is all powerful to do good, and at the same time is restrain'd from committing evil; where the Nobles are great without insolence, tho' there are no Vassals; and where the People share in the government without confusion.

THE house of Lords and that of the Commons divide the legislative power under the King, but the *Romans* had no such balance. The Patricians and Plebeians in *Rome* were perpetually at variance, and there was no intermediate Power to reconcile them. The *Roman* Senate who were so unjustly, so criminally proud, as not to suffer the Plebeians to share with them in any thing, cou'd find no other artifice to keep the latter out of the Administration than by employing them in foreign wars. They consider'd the Plebeians as a wild beast, whom it behov'd them to let loose upon their neighbours, for fear they should devour their masters. Thus the greatest defect in the Government of the *Romans* rais'd 'em to be Conquerors. By being unhappy at home, they triumph'd over, and possess'd themselves of the world, till at last their divisions sunk them to Slavery.

THE government of *England* will never rise to so exalted a pitch of glory, nor will its end be so fatal. The *English* are not fir'd with the splendid folly of making conquests, but would only prevent their neighbours from conquering. They are not only jealous of their own Liberty, but even of that of other nations. The *English* were exasperated against *Lewis* the Fourteenth, for no other reason but because he was ambitious; and declar'd war against him merely out of levity, not from any interested motives.

T H E *English* have doubtless purchas'd their Liberties at a very high price, and waded thro' seas of blood to drown the Idol of arbitrary Power. Other nations have been involv'd in as great calamities, and have shed as much blood; but then the blood they spilt in defence of their Liberties, only enslaved them the more.

T H A T which rises to a Revolution in *England* is no more than a Sedition in other countries. A city in *Spain*, in *Barbary*, or in *Turkey*, takes up arms in defence of its Privileges, when immediately 'tis storm'd by mercenary Troops, 'tis punish'd by Executioners, and the rest of the Nation kiss the chains they are loaded with. The *French* are of opinion, that the government of this Island is more tempestuous than the sea which surrounds it, which indeed is true; but then 'tis never so but when the King raises the storm; when he attempts to seize the Ship of which he is only the chief Pilot. The civil wars of *France* lasted longer; were more cruel, and productive of greater evils than those of *England*: But none of these civil Wars had a wise and prudent Liberty for their object.

I N the detestable Reigns of *Charles* the ninth, and *Henry* the third, the whole affair was only whether the people should be slaves to the *Guises*. With regard to the last war of *Paris*, it deserves only to be hooted at. Methinks I see a croud of

School-boys rising up in arms against their Master, and afterwards whipp'd for it. Cardinal *de Retz*, who was witty and brave, but to no purpose; rebellious without a cause; factious without design, and head of a defenceless Party, caball'd for caballing sake, and seem'd to foment the civil War merely out of diversion. The Parliament did not know what he intended, nor what he did not intend. He levied troops by act of Parliament, and the next moment cashier'd them. He threatned, he begg'd pardon; he set a price upon Cardinal *Mazarine's* head, and afterwards congratulated him in a public manner. Our civil wars under *Charles* the sixth were bloody and cruel, those of the *League* execrable, and that of the * *Frondeurs* ridiculous.

THAT for which the *French* chiefly reproach the *English* Nation, is, the murther of King *Charles* the First, whom his subjects treated exactly as he wou'd have treated them, had his Reign been prosperous. After all, consider on one side, *Charles* the first defeated in a pitch'd battle, imprison'd, try'd, sentenc'd to die in *Westminster-hall*, and then beheaded: And on the other, the Emperor *Henry* the seventh, poison'd by his chaplain at his receiving the sacrament; *Henry* the third stabb'd by a Monk;

* *Frondeurs*, in its proper sense *Slingers*, and figuratively *Cavillers*, or lovers of contradiction; was a name given to a league or party that oppos'd the *French* ministry, *i.e.* Cardinal *Mazarine* in 1648. See *Rochefault's* Memoirs.

thirty assassinations projected against *Henry* the fourth; several of them put in execution, and the last bereaving that great Monarch of his life. Weigh, I say, all these wicked attempts, and then judge.

LETTER IX.

ON THE

GOVERNMENT.

THAT mixture in the *English* government, that harmony between King, Lords and Commons, did not always subsist. *England* was enslav'd for a long series of years by the *Romans*, the *Saxons*, the *Danes*, and the *French* successively. *William* the conqueror particularly rul'd them with a rod of iron. He dispos'd as absolutely of the lives and fortunes of his conquer'd subjects as an eastern Monarch; and forbid, upon pain of death, the *English* both fire or candle in their houses after eight a clock; whether he did this to prevent their nocturnal meetings, or only to try, by this odd and whimsical prohibition, how far it was possible for one Man to extend his power over his fellow Creatures. 'Tis true indeed that the *English* had Parliaments before and after *William* the Conqueror; and they boast of them, as tho' these assemblies then call'd Parliaments, compos'd of ecclesiastical Tyrants, and of plunderers entitled Barons, had been the guardians of the publick liberty and happiness.

T H E Barbarians who came from the shores of the *Baltick*, and settled in the rest of *Europe*, brought with them the form of government call'd States or Parliaments, about which so much noise is made, and which are so little understood. Kings indeed were not absolute in those days, but then the people were more wretched upon that very account, and more completely enslav'd. The Chiefs of these savages who had laid waste *France*, *Italy*, *Spain* and *England*, made themselves Monarchs. Their generals divided among themselves the several countries they had conquer'd, whence sprung those Margraves, those Peers, those Barons, those petty Tyrants, who often contested with their Sovereigns for the spoils of whole nations. These were birds of prey, fighting with an Eagle for Doves, whose blood the Victorious was to suck. Every nation, instead of being govern'd by one Master, was trampled upon by an hundred Tyrants. The priests soon play'd a part among them. Before this, it had been the fate of the *Gauls*, the *Germans* and the *Britons*, to be always govern'd by their Druids, and the Chiefs of their villages, an ancient kind of Barons, not so tyrannical as their successors. These Druids pretended to be mediators between God and man. They enacted laws, they fulminated their excommunications, and sentenc'd to death. The Bishops succeeded, by insensible degrees, to their temporal authority in the *Goth* and *Vandal* government. The Popes set themselves at their head, and arm'd with their Briefs, their Bulls, and reinforc'd by Monks, they made even Kings tremble; depos'd and assassinated them at pleasure, and employ'd every artifice to draw into their own purses, monies from all parts of *Europe*. The weak *Ina*, one of the tyrants of the *Saxon* Heptarchy in *England*, was the first Monarch that submitted, in his pilgrimage to *Rome*, to pay St. *Peter's* penny (equivalent very near to a *French* crown) for every house in his dominions. The whole Island soon follow'd his example; *England* became insensibly one of the Pope's provinces, and the holy Father us'd to send from time to time his Legates thither to levy exorbitant taxes. At last King *John* deliver'd up by a public instrument, the Kingdom of *England* to the Pope, who had excommunicated him; but the Barons not finding their account in this resignation, dethron'd the wretched King *John* and seated *Lewis*, father to St. *Lewis* King of *France* in his place. However they were soon weary of their new Monarch, and accordingly oblig'd him to return back to *France*.

WHILST that the Barons, the Bishops, and the Popes, all laid waste *England*, where all were for ruling; the most numerous, the most useful, even the most virtuous, and consequently the

most venerable part of mankind, consisting
of those who study the laws and the sciences;
of traders, of artificers, in a word, of all
who were not tyrants; that is, those who are
call'd the people; these, I say, were by them
look'd upon as so many animals beneath the
dignity of the human species. The Commons in
those ages were far from sharing in the government, they being *Villains* or Peasants whose
labour, whose blood were the property of their
Masters who entitled themselves the Nobility.
The major part of men in *Europe* were at that
time what they are to this day in several parts
of the world, they were *Villains* or Bondsmen
of Lords, that is, a kind of cattle bought and sold
with the land. Many ages past away before
justice cou'd be done to human nature; before
mankind were conscious, that 'twas abominable
numbers should sow, and but few reap: And
was not *France* very happy, when the power
and authority of those petty Robbers was abolish'd by the lawful authority of Kings and of the
People?

H A P P I L Y in the violent shocks which the
divisions between Kings and the Nobles gave
to empires, the chains of Nations were more or
less heavy. Liberty, in *England*, sprung from
the quarrels of Tyrants. The Barons forc'd
King *John* and King *Henry* the third, to grant
the famous *Magna Charta*, the chief design of
which was indeed to make Kings dependant on

the Lords, but then the rest of the nation were
a little favour'd in it, in order that they might
join, on proper occasions, with their pretended
Masters. This great Charter which is consider'd
as the sacred origin of the *English* Liberties,
shews in it self how little Liberty was known.

THE Title alone proves, that the King thought
he had a just right to be absolute; and that the
Barons, and even the Clergy forc'd him to give
up that pretended right, for no other reason
but because they were the most powerful.

MAGNA CHARTA begins in this stile,
*We grant, of our own free will, the following
Privileges to the Archbishops, Bishops, Priors and
Barons of our Kingdom,* &c.

THE House of Commons is not once mention'd in the Articles of this Charter, a Proof
that it did not yet exist, or that it existed without Power. Mention is therein made, by name,
of the Freemen of *England*, a melancholy Proof
that some were not so. It appears by the thirty
second Article, that these pretended Freemen
ow'd Service to their Lords. Such a Liberty as
this, was not many removes from Slavery.

BY article XXI, the King ordains that his
Officers shall not henceforward seize upon, unless they pay for them, the Horses and Carts of
Freemen. The people consider'd this Ordinance
as a real Liberty, tho' it was a greater Tyranny.
Henry the seventh, that happy Usurper and
great Politician, who pretended to love the Barons,

tho' he in reality hated and fear'd them, got their Lands alienated. By this means the *Villains*, afterwards acquiring Riches by their Industry, purchas'd the Estates and Country-Seats of the illustrious Peers who had ruin'd themselves by their Folly and Extravagance, and all the Lands got by insensible Degrees into other Hands.

T H E Power of the House of Commons increas'd every Day. The Families of the ancient Peers were at last extinct; and as Peers only are properly noble in *England*, there would be no such thing in strictness of Law, as Nobility in that Island, had not the Kings created new Barons from Time to Time, and preserv'd the Body of Peers, once a Terror to them, to oppose them to the Commons since become so formidable.

A L L these new Peers who compose the higher House, receive nothing but their Titles from the King, and very few of them have Estates in those Places whence they take their Titles. One shall be Duke of *D*—— tho' he has not a Foot of Land in *Dorsetshire*; and another is Earl of a Village, tho' he scarce knows where it is situated. The Peers have Power, but 'tis only in the Parliament House.

T H E R E is no such thing here, as **haute*,

* *La haute justice*, is that of a Lord, who has Power to sentence capitally, and to judge of all Causes civil and criminal, those of the Crown excepted. *La moyenne justice*, is empower'd to judge of Actions relating to Guardianships, and Offences. *La basse justice* takes Cognizance of the Fees

moyenne, & basse justice, that is, a Power to
judge in all Matters civil and criminal; nor a
Right or Privilege of Hunting in the Grounds
of a Citizen, who at the same time is not permitted to fire a Gun in his own Field.

N o one is exempted in this Country from
paying certain Taxes, because he is a Nobleman
or a Priest. All Duties and Taxes are settled by
the House of Commons, whose Power is greater
than that of the Peers, tho' inferiour to it in dignity. The spiritual as well as temporal Lords
have the Liberty to reject a Money Bill brought
in by the Commons, but they are not allow'd to
alter any thing in it, and must either pass or
throw it out without Restriction. When the Bill
has pass'd the Lords and is sign'd by the King,
then the whole Nation pays, every Man in proportion to his Revenue or Estate, not according
to his Title, which would be absurd. There is
no such thing as an arbitrary Subsidy or Poll-
Tax, but a real Tax on the Lands, of all which
an Estimate was made in the Reign of the famous
King *William* the Third.

T H E Land-Tax continues still upon the
same foot, tho' the Revenue of the Lands is
increas'd. Thus no one is tyranniz'd over, and
every one is easy. The Feet of the Peasants are
not bruis'd by wooden Shoes; they eat white

due to the Lord, of the Havock of Beasts, and of Offences.
The *moyenne justice* is imaginary, and there is perhaps no
Instance of its ever being put in Execution.

Bread, are well cloath'd, and are not afraid of increasing their Stock of Cattle, nor of tiling their Houses, from any Apprehensions that their Taxes will be rais'd the Year following. The annual Income of the Estates of a great many Commoners in *England*, amounts to two hundred thousand Livres; and yet these don't think it beneath them to plough the Lands which enrich them, and on which they enjoy their Liberty.

LETTER X.

ON

TRADE.

As Trade enrich'd the Citizens in *England*, so it contributed to their Freedom, and this Freedom on the other Side extended their Commerce, whence arose the Grandeur of the State. Trade rais'd by insensible Degrees the naval Power, which gives the *English* a Superiority over the Seas, and they are now Masters of very near two hundred Ships of War. Posterity will very possibly be surpriz'd to hear that an Island whose only Produce is a little Lead, Tin, Fuller's Earth, and coarse Wood, should become so powerful by its Commerce, as to be able to send in 1723, three Fleets at the same Time to three different and far distanc'd Parts of the Globe. One before *Gibraltar*, conquer'd and still possess'd by the *English*; a second to *Porto Bello*, to dispossess the King of *Spain* of the Treasures of the *West-Indies*; and a third into the *Baltick*, to prevent the *Northern* Powers from coming to an Engagement.

A t the Time when *Lewis* XIV made all *Italy* tremble, and that his Armies, which had already possess'd themselves of *Savoy* and *Piedmont*, were upon the Point of taking *Turin*; Prince *Eugene* was oblig'd to march from the Middle of *Germany* in order to succour *Savoy*. Having no Money, without which Cities cannot be either taken or defended, he address'd himself to some *English* Merchants. These, at an Hour and half's Warning, lent him five Millions, whereby he was enabled to deliver *Turin*, and to beat the *French*; after which he wrote the following short Letter to the Persons who had disburs'd him the abovemention'd Sums: " Gen-" tlemen, I have receiv'd your Money, and flatter " my self that I have laid it out to your Satis-faction." Such a Circumstance as this raises a just Pride in an *English* Merchant, and makes him presume (not without some Reason) to compare himself to a *Roman* Citizen; and indeed a Peer's Brother does not think Traffic beneath him. When the Lord *Townshend* was Minister of State, a Brother of his was content to be a City Merchant; and at the Time that the Earl of *Oxford* govern'd *Great-Britain*, his younger Brother was no more than a Factor in *Aleppo*, where he chose to live, and where he died. This Custom, which begins however to be laid aside, appears monstruous to *Germans*, vainly puff'd up with their Extraction. These think it morally impossible that the Son of an *English* Peer should be no more than a rich and powerful Citizens, for all are Princes in *Germany*. There have been thirty Highnesses of the same Name, all whose Patrimony consisted only in their Escutcheons and their Pride.

IN *France* the Title of Marquis is given *gratis* to any one who will accept of it; and whosoever arrives at *Paris* from the midst of the most remote Provinces with Money in his Purse, and a Name terminating in *ac* or *ille*, may strut about, and cry, such a Man as I! A Man of my Rank and Figure! And may look down upon a Trader with sovereign Contempt; whilst the Trader on the other Side, by thus often hearing his Profession treated so disdainfully, is Fool enough to blush at it. However, I cannot say which is most useful to a Nation; a Lord, powder'd in the tip of the Mode, who knows exactly at what a Clock the King rises and goes to bed; and who gives himself Airs of Grandeur and State, at the same Time that he is acting the Slave in the Anti-chamber of a prime Minister; or a Merchant, who enriches his Country, dispatches Orders from his Compting-House to *Surat* and *Grand Cairo*, and contributes to the Felicity of the World.

LETTER XI.

ON

INOCULATION.

IT is inadvertently affirm'd in the Christian Countries of *Europe*, that the *English* are Fools and Madmen. Fools, because they give their Children the Small-Pox to prevent their catching it; and Mad-men, because they wantonly communicate a certain and dreadful Distemper to their Children, merely to prevent an uncertain Evil. The *English*, on the other Side, call the rest of the *Europeans* cowardly and unnatural. Cowardly, because they are afraid of putting their Children to a little Pain; unnatural, because they expose them to die one Time or other of the Small-Pox. But that the Reader may be able to judge, whether the *English* or those who differ from them in opinion, are in the right, here follows the History of the fam'd Inoculation, which is mention'd with so much Dread in *France*.

THE *Circassian* Women have, from Time

immemorial, communicated the Small-Pox to
their Children when not above six Months old,
by making an Incision in the arm, and by putting
into this Incision a Pustle, taken carefully from
the Body of another Child. This Pustle produces the same Effect in the arm it is laid in, as
Yest in a Piece of Dough: It ferments, and dif-
fuses through the whole Mass of Blood, the
Qualities with which it is impregnated. The
Pustles of the Child, in whom the artificial
Small-Pox has been thus inoculated, are employ'd to communicate the same Distemper to
others. There is an almost perpetual Circulation
of it in *Circassia*; and when unhappily the Small-
Pox has quite left the Country, the Inhabitants
of it are in as great Trouble and Perplexity, as
other Nations when their Harvest has fallen
short.

T h e Circumstance that introduc'd a Custom
in *Circassia*, which appears so singular to others,
is nevertheless a Cause common to all Nations,
I mean maternal Tenderness and Interest.

T h e *Circassians* are poor, and their Daugh-
ters are beautiful, and indeed 'tis in them they
chiefly trade. They furnish with Beauties, the
Seraglios of the *Turkish* Sultan, of the *Persian*
Sophy, and of all those who are wealthy enough
to purchase and maintain such precious Mer-
chandize. These Maidens are very honourably
and virtuously instructed to fondle and caress
Men; are taught Dances of a very polite and

effeminate kind; and how to heighten by the
most voluptuous Artifices, the Pleasures of their
disdainful Masters for whom they are design'd.
These unhappy Creatures repeat their Lesson
to their Mothers, in the same manner as little
Girls among us repeat their Catechism, without
understanding one Word they say.

N o w it often happen'd, that after a Father
and Mother had taken the utmost Care of the
Education of their Children, they were frustrated
of all their Hopes in an Instant. The Small-Pox
getting into the Family, one Daughter died of
it, another lost an Eye, a third had a great Nose
at her Recovery, and the unhappy Parents were
completely ruin'd. Even frequently, when the
Small-Pox became epidemical, Trade was sus-
pended for several Years, which thinn'd very
considerably the Seraglios of *Persia* and *Turkey*.

A TRADING Nation is always watchful
over its own Interests, and grasps at every Discovery that may be of Advantage to its Commerce. The *Circassians* observ'd, that scarce
one Person in a Thousand was ever attack'd by
a Small Pox of a violent kind. That some indeed
had this Distemper very favourably three or
four Times, but never twice so as to prove fatal;
in a Word, that no one ever had it in a violent
Degree twice in his Life. They observ'd farther, that when the Small-Pox is of the milder
Sort, and the Pustles have only a tender, delicate
Skin to break thro', they never leave the least

Scar in the Face. From these natural Observations they concluded, that in case an Infant of six Months or a Year old, should have a milder Sort of Small-Pox, he wou'd not die of it, would not be mark'd, nor be ever afflicted with it again.

IN order therefore to preserve the Life and Beauty of their Children, the only Thing remaining was, to give them the Small-Pox in their infant Years. This they did, by inoculating in the Body of a Child, a Pustle taken from the most regular, and at the same Time the most favourable Sort of Small-Pox that could be procur'd.

THE Experiment cou'd not possibly fail. The *Turks*, who are People of good Sense, soon adopted this Custom, insomuch that at this Time there is not a Bassa in *Constantinople*, but communicates the Small-Pox to his Children of both Sexes, immediately upon their being wean'd.

SOME pretend, that the *Circassians* borrow'd this Custom anciently from the *Arabians*; but we shall leave the clearing up of this Point of History to some learned Benedictine, who will not fail to compile a great many Folio's on this Subject, with the several Proofs or Authorities. All I have to say upon it, is, that in the beginning of the Reign of King *George* the First, the Lady *Wortley Mountague*, a Woman of as fine a Genius, and endu'd with as great a Strength of Mind, as any of her Sex in the *British* Kingdoms, being with her Husband who was Ambassador at the Port, made no scruple to communicate the Small-Pox to an Infant of which she was deliver'd in *Constantinople*. The Chaplain represented to his Lady, but to no purpose, that this was an unchristian Operation, and therefore that it cou'd succeed with none but Infidels. However, it had the most happy Effect upon the Son of the Lady *Wortley Mountague*, who, at her Return to *England*, communicated the Experiment to the Princess of *Wales*, now Queen of *England*. It must be confess'd that this Princess, abstracted from her Crown and Titles, was born to encourage the whole Circle of Arts, and to do good to Mankind. She appears as an amiable Philosopher on the Throne, having never let slip one Opportunity of improving the great Talents she receiv'd from Nature, nor of exerting her Beneficence. 'Tis she, who being inform'd that a Daughter of *Milton* was living, but in miserable Circumstances, immediately sent her a considerable Present. 'Tis she who protects the learned Father *Courayer*. 'Tis she who condescended to attempt a Reconciliation between Dr. *Clark* and Mr. *Leibnitz*. The Moment this Princess heard of Inoculation, she caus'd an Experiment of it to be made on four Criminals sentenced to die, and by that means preserv'd their Lives doubly; for she not only sav'd them from the Gallows, but by means of this artificial Small-Pox, prevented their ever having that Distemper in a natural Way, with which they would very probably have been attack'd one Time or other, and might have died of in a more advanc'd Age.

THE Princess being assur'd of the Usefulness of this Operation, caus'd her own Children to be inoculated. A great Part of the Kingdom follow'd her Example, and since that Time ten thousand Children, at least, of Persons of Condition owe in this Manner their Lives to her Majesty, and to the Lady *Wortley Mountague*; and as many of the Fair Sex are oblig'd to them for their Beauty.

UPON a general Calculation, threescore Persons in every hundred have the Small-Pox. Of these threescore, twenty die of it in the most favourable Season of Life, and as many more wear the disagreeable Remains of it in their Faces so long as they live. Thus, a fifth Part of Mankind either die, or are disfigur'd by this Distemper. But it does not prove fatal to so much as one, among those who are inoculated in *Turkey* or in *England*, unless the Patient be infirm, or would have died had not the Experiment been made upon him. Besides, no one is disfigur'd, no one has the Small-Pox a second Time, if the Inoculation was perfect. 'Tis therefore certain, that had the Lady of some *French* Ambassador brought this Secret from *Constantinople* to *Paris*, the Nation would have been for ever oblig'd to her. Then the Duke *de Ville-quier*, Father to the Duke *d'Aumont*, who enjoys the most vigorous Constitution, and is the healthiest Man in *France*, would not have been cut off in the Flower of.his Age.

T H E Prince of *Soubise*, happy in the finest Flush of Health, would not have been snatch'd away at five and twenty; nor the Dauphin, Grandfather to *Lewis* the Fifteenth, have been laid in his Grave in his fiftieth Year. Twenty thousand Persons whom the Small-Pox swept away at *Paris* in 1723, would have been alive at this Time. But are not the *French* fond of Life, and is Beauty so inconsiderable an Advantage as to be disregarded by the Ladies! It must be confess'd that we are an odd kind of People. Perhaps our Nation will imitate, ten Years hence, this Practice of the *English*, if the Clergy and the Physicians will but give them Leave to do it : Or possibly our Country Men may introduce Inoculation three Months hence in *France* out of mere whim, in case the *English* should discontinue it thro' Fickleness.

I A M inform'd that the *Chinese* have practis'd Inoculation these hundred Years, a Circumstance that argues very much in its Favour, since they are thought to be the wisest and best govern'd People in the World. The *Chinese* indeed don't communicate this Distemper by Inoculation, but at the Nose, in the same Manner as we take Snuff. This is a more agreeable way, but then it produces the like Effects; and proves at the same Time, that had Inoculation been practis'd in *France*, 'twould have sav'd the Lives of Thousands.

L E T T E R   XII.

O N   T H E

Lord *BACON*.

N o t long since, the trite and frivolous Question following was debated in a very polite and learned Company, *viz.* who was the greatest Man, *Cæsar*, *Alexander*, *Tamerlane*, *Cromwell*, &c.

S o m e Body answer'd, that Sir *Isaac Newton* excell'd them all. The Gentleman's Assertion was very just; for if true Greatness consists in having receiv'd from Heaven a mighty Genius, and in having employ'd it to enlighten our own Minds and that of others; a Man like Sir *Isaac Newton*, whose equal is hardly found in a thousand Years, is the truly great Man. And those Politicians and Conquerors, (and all ages produce some) were generally so many illustrious wicked Men. That Man claims our Respect, who commands over the Minds of the rest of the World by the Force of Truth, not those who enslave their Fellow Creatures; He who is acquainted with the Universe, not They who deface it.

SINCE therefore you desire me to give you an Account of the famous Personages which *England* has given birth to, I shall begin with Lord *Bacon*, Mr. *Locke*, Sir *Isaac Newton*, *&c.* Afterwards the Warriors and Ministers of State shall come in their order.

I MUST begin with the celebrated Viscount *Verulam*, known in *Europe* by the Name of *Bacon*, which was that of his Family, His Father had been Lord Keeper, and himself was a great many Years Lord Chancellor under King *James* the First. Nevertheless, amidst the Intrigues of a Court, and the Affairs of his exalted Employment, which alone were enough to engross his whole Time, he yet found so much Leisure for Study, as to make himself a great Philosopher, a good Historian, and an elegant Writer; and a still more surprizing Circumstance is, that he liv'd in an Age in which the Art of writing justly and elegantly was little known, much less true Philosophy. Lord *Bacon*, as is the Fate of Man, was more esteem'd after his Death than in his Life-time. His Enemies were in the *British* Court, and his Admirers were Foreigners.

WHEN the Marquis *d'Effiat* attended in *England* upon the Princess *Henrietta Maria*, Daughter to *Henry* the Fourth, whom King *Charles* the First had married, that Minister went and visited the Lord *Bacon*, who being at

that Time sick in his Bed, receiv'd him with the
Curtains shut close. You resemble the Angels,
says the Marquis to him; we hear those Beings
spoken of perpetually, and we believe them
superior to Men, but are never allow'd the Con-
solation to see them.

Y o u know that this great Man was accus'd
of a Crime very unbecoming a Philosopher, I
mean Bribery and Extortion. You know that
he was sentenc'd by the House of Lords, to pay
a Fine of about four hundred thousand *French*
Livres; to lose his Peerage and his Dignity of
Chancellor. But in the present Age, the *English*
revere his Memory to such a Degree, that they
will scarce allow him to have been guilty. In
case you should ask what are my Thoughts on
this Head, I shall answer you in the Words
which I heard the Lord *Bolingbroke* use on another Occasion. Several Gentlemen were speaking, in his Company, of the Avarice with which
the late Duke of *Marlborough* had been charg'd,
some Examples whereof being given, the Lord
Bolingbroke was appeal'd to, (who having been
in the opposite Party, might perhaps, without
the Imputation of Indecency, have been allow'd
to clear up that Matter:) " He was so great a
" Man, replied his Lordship, that I have forgot
" his Vices."

I s h a l l therefore confine my self to those
Things which so justly gain'd Lord *Bacon* the
Esteem of all *Europe*.

T H E most singular, and the best of all his Pieces, is that which, at this Time, is the most useless and the least read, I mean his *Novum Scientiarum Organum*. This is the Scaffold with which the new Philosophy was rais'd; and when the Edifice was built, Part of it at least, the Scaffold was no longer of Service.

T H E Lord *Bacon* was not yet acquainted with Nature, but then he knew, and pointed out, the several Paths that lead to it. He had despis'd in his younger Years the Thing call'd Philosophy in the Universities; and did all that lay in his Power to prevent those Societies of Men, instituted to improve human Reason, from depraving it by their Quiddities, their Horrors of the *Vacuum*, their substantial Forms, and all those impertinent Terms which not only Ignorance had rendred venerable, but which had been sacred, by their being ridiculously blended with Religion.

H E is the Father of experimental Philosophy. It must indeed be confess'd, that very surprizing Secrets had been found out before his Time. The Sea-Compass, Printing, engraving on Copper Plates, Oil-Painting, Looking-Glasses; the Art of restoring, in some Measure, old Men to their Sight by Spectacles; Gun-Powder, *&c.* had been discover'd. A new World had been sought for, found, and conquer'd. Would not one suppose that these sublime Discoveries had been made by the greatest Philosophers, and in Ages much more enlightened than the present? But 'twas far otherwise; all these great Changes happen'd in the most stupid and barbarous Times. Chance only gave Birth to most of those Inventions; and 'tis very probable that what is call'd Chance, contributed very much to the Discovery of *America*; at least it has been always thought, that *Christopher Columbus* undertook his Voyage, merely on the Relation of a Captain of a Ship, which a Storm had drove as far Westward as the *Caribee* Islands. Be this as it will, Men had sail'd round the World, and cou'd destroy Cities by an artificial Thunder more dreadful than the real one: But, then they were not acquainted with the Circulation of the Blood, the Weight of the Air, the Laws of Motion, Light, the Number of our Planets, *&c.* And a Man who maintain'd a Thesis on *Aristotle's* Categories; on the universals *a parte rei*, or such like Nonsense, was look'd upon as a Prodigy.

T H E most astonishing, the most useful Inventions, are not those which reflect the greatest Honour on the human Mind. 'Tis to a mechanical Instinct, which is found in many Men, and not to true Philosophy, that most Arts owe their Origin.

T H E discovery of Fire, the Art of making Bread, of melting and preparing Metals, of building Houses, and the Invention of the Shuttle, are infinitely more beneficial to Mankind then Printing or the Sea-Compass: And yet these Arts were invented by uncultivated, savage Men.

WHAT a prodigious use the *Greeks* and *Romans* made afterwards of Mechanicks! Nevertheless, they believ'd that there were crystal Heavens; that the Stars were small Lamps which sometimes fell into the Sea; and one of their greatest Philosophers, after long Researches found that the Stars were so many Flints which had been detach'd from the Earth.

IN a Word, no one, before the Lord *Bacon*, was acquainted with experimental Philosophy, nor with the several physical Experiments which have been made since his Time. Scarce one of them but is hinted at in his Work, and he himself had made several. He made a kind of pneumatic Engine, by which he guess'd the elasticity of the Air. He approach'd, on all Sides as it were, to the Discovery of its Weight, and had very near attain'd it, but some Time after *Toricelli* seiz'd upon this Truth. In a little Time experimental Philosophy began to be cultivated on a sudden in most Parts of *Europe*. 'Twas a hidden Treasure which the Lord *Bacon* had some Notion of, and which all the Philosophers, encourag'd by his Promises, endeavour'd to dig up.

BUT that which surpriz'd me most was to read in his Work, in express Terms, the new Attraction, the Invention of which is ascrib'd to Sir *Isaac Newton*.

WE must search, says Lord *Bacon*, whether there may not be a kind of magnetic Power, which operates between the Earth and heavy Bodies, between the Moon and the Ocean, between the Planets, &c. In another Place he says, either heavy Bodies must be carried towards the Center of the Earth, or must be reciprocally attracted by it; and in the latter Case 'tis evident, that the nearer Bodies, in their falling, draw towards the Earth, the stronger they will attract one another. We must, says he, make an Experiment to see whether the same Clock will go faster on the Top of a Mountain or at the Bottom of a Mine. Whether the Strength of the Weights decreases on the Mountain, and increases in the Mine. 'Tis probable that the Earth has a true attractive Power.

THIS Fore-runner in Philosophy was also an elegant Writer, an Historian and a Wit.

HIS moral Essays are greatly esteem'd, but they were drawn up in the View of instructing rather than of pleasing: And as they are not a Satyr upon Mankind, like *Rochefoucaults's* Maxims, nor written upon a sceptical Plan, like *Montagne's* Essays, they are not so much read as those two ingenious Authors.

HIS History of *Henry* the Seventh was look'd upon as a Master-Piece, but how is it possible that some Persons can presume to compare so little a Work with the History of our illustrious *Thuanus?*

SPEAKING about the famous Impostor *Perkin*, Son to a converted * *Jew*, who assum'd boldly the Name and Title of *Richard* the Fourth, King of *England*, at the Instigation of the Duchess of *Burgundy*; and who disputed the Crown with *Henry* the Seventh, the Lord *Bacon* writes as follows:

" AT this Time the King began again to be
" haunted with Sprites, by the Magick and
" curious Arts of the Lady *Margaret*; who raised
" up the Ghost of *Richard* Duke of *York*, second
" Son to King *Edward* the Fourth, to walk and
" vex the King."†

" AFTER such Time as she (*Margaret* of
" *Burgundy*) thought he (*Perkin Warbeck*) was
" perfect in his Lesson, she began to cast with
" her self from what Coast this *Blazing-Starre*
" should first appear, and at what Time it must
" be upon the Horizon of *Ireland*; for there
" had the like Meteor strong Influence before."‡

METHINKS our sagacious *Thuanus* does not give into such Fustian, which formerly was look'd upon as Sublime, but in this Age is justly call'd Nonsense.

* *John Osbeck.*

† The History of the Reign of King *Henry* the Seventh, *page* 112. *London*, printed in 1641. Folio.

‡ Idem. *p.* 116.

LETTER XIII.

ON

Mr. *L O C K E.*

PERHAPS no Man ever had a more judicious or more methodical Genius, or was a more acute Logician than Mr. *Locke*, and yet he was not deeply skill'd in the Mathematicks. This great Man could never subject himself to the tedious Fatigue of Calculations, nor to the dry Pursuit of Mathematical Truths, which do not at first present any sensible Objects to the Mind; and no one has given better Proofs than he, that 'tis possible for a Man to have a geometrical Head without the Assistance of Geometry. Before his Time, several great Philosophers had declar'd, in the most positive Terms, what the Soul of Man is; but as these absolutely knew nothing about it, they might very well be allow'd to differ entirely in opinion from one another.

IN *Greece*, the infant Seat of Arts and of Errors, and where the Grandeur as well as

Folly of the human Mind went such prodigious Lengths, the People us'd to reason about the Soul in the very same Manner as we do.

T H E divine *Anaxagoras*, in whose Honour an Altar was erected, for his having taught Mankind that the Sun was greater than *Peloponnesus*, that Snow was black, and that the Heavens were of Stone; affirm'd that the Soul was an aerial Spirit, but at the same Time immortal. *Diogenes*, (not he who was a cyncial Philosopher after having coyn'd base Money) declar'd that the Soul was a Portion of the Substance of God; an Idea which we must confess was very sublime. *Epicurus* maintain'd that it was compos'd of Parts in the same Manner as the Body.

A R I S T O T L E who has been explain'd a thousand Ways, because he is unintelligible, was of Opinion, according to some of his Disciples, that the Understanding in all Men is one and the same Substance.

T H E divine *Plato*, Master of the divine *Aristotle*, and the divine *Socrates* Master of the divine *Plato*, us'd to say that the Soul was corporeal and eternal. No doubt but the Demon of *Socrates* had instructed him in the Nature of it. Some People, indeed, pretend, that a Man who boasted his being attended by a familiar Genius, must infallibly be either a Knave or a Madman, but this kind of People are seldom satisfied with any Thing but Reason.

WITH regard to the Fathers of the Church, several in the primitive Ages believ'd that the Soul was human, and the Angels and God corporeal. Men naturally improve upon every System, St. *Bernard*, as Father *Mabillon* confesses, taught that the Soul after Death does not see God in the celestial Regions, but converses with *Christ's* human Nature only. However, he was not believ'd this Time on his bare Word; the Adventure of the Crusade having a little sunk the Credit of his Oracles. Afterwards a thousand Schoolmen arose, such as the irrefragable* Doctor, the subtil Doctor †, the angelic Doctor ‡, the seraphic Doctor ‖, and the cherubic Doctor, who were all sure that they had a very clear and distinct Idea of the Soul, and yet wrote in such a Manner, that one would conclude they were resolv'd no one should understand a Word in their Writings. Our *Des Cartes*, born not to discover the Errors of Antiquity, but to substitute his own in the Room of them; and hurried away by that systematic Spirit which throws a Cloud over the Minds of the greatest Men, thought he had demonstrated that the Soul is the same Thing as Thought, in the same Manner as Matter, in his Opinion, is the same as Extension. He asserted, that Man thinks eternally, and that the Soul, at its coming into the Body, is inform'd with the whole Series of

* *Alexander de Hales.* † *Duns Scotus.* ‡ St. *Thomas.* ‖ St. *Bonaventure.*

metaphysical Notions; knowing God, infinite Space, possessing all abstract Ideas; in a Word, completely endued with the most sublime Lights, which it unhappily forgets at its issuing from the Womb.

F A T H E R *Malbranche,* in his sublime Illusions, not only admitted innate Ideas, but did not doubt of our living wholly in God, and that God is, as it were, our Soul.

S U C H a Multitude of Reasoners having written the Romance of the Soul, a Sage at last arose, who gave, with an Air of the greatest Modesty, the History of it. Mr. *Locke* has display'd the human Soul, in the same Manner as an excellent Anatomist explains the Springs of the human Body. He every where takes the Light of Physicks for his Guide. He sometimes presumes to speak affirmatively, but then he presumes also to doubt. Instead of concluding at once what we know not, he examines gradually what we wou'd know. He takes an Infant at the Instant of his Birth; he traces, Step by Step, the Progress of his Understanding; examines what Things he has in common with Beasts, and what he possesses above them. Above all he consults himself; the being conscious that he himself thinks.

I S H A L L leave, says he, to those who know more of this Matter than my self, the examining whether the Soul exists before or after the Organization of our Bodies. But I confess that

'tis my Lot to be animated with one of those
heavy Souls which do not think always; and I
am even so unhappy as not to conceive, that 'tis
more necessary the Soul should think perpetually,
than that Bodies shou'd be for ever in Motion.

WITH regard to my self, I shall boast that
I have the Honour to be as stupid in this Particular as Mr. *Locke*. No one shall ever make me
believe, that I think always; and I am as little
inclin'd as he cou'd be, to fancy that some Weeks
after I was conceiv'd, I was a very learned Soul;
knowing at that Time a thousand Things which
I forgot at my Birth; and possessing when in the
Womb, (tho' to no Manner of Purpose), Knowledge which I lost the Instant I had occasion
for it; and which I have never since been able
to recover perfectly.

MR. LOCKE after having destroy'd innate
Ideas; after having fully renounc'd the Vanity
of believing that we think always; after having
laid down, from the most solid Principles, that
Ideas enter the Mind through the Senses; having examin'd our simple and complex Ideas;
having trac'd the human Mind through its
several Operations; having shew'd that all the
Languages in the World are imperfect, and the
great Abuse that is made of Words every Moment; he at last comes to consider the Extent
or rather the narrow Limits of human Knowledge. 'Twas in this Chapter he presum'd to
advance, but very modestly, the following Words,

" We shall, perhaps, never be capable of know-
" ing, whether a Being, purely material, thinks
" or not." This sage Assertion was, by more
Divines than one, look'd upon as a scandalous
Declaration that the Soul is material and mortal.
Some *Englishmen*, devout after their Way,
sounded an Alarm. The Superstitious are the
same in Society as Cowards in an Army; they
themselves are seiz'd with a panic Fear, and
communicate it to others. 'Twas loudly exclaim'd, that Mr. *Locke* intended to destroy
Religion; nevertheless, Religion had nothing
to do in the Affair, it being a Question purely
Philosophical, altogether independent on Faith
and Revelation. Mr. *Locke's* Opponents needed
but to examine, calmly and impartially, whether
the declaring that Matter can think, implies a
Contradiction; and whether God is able to
communicate Thought to Matter. But Divines
are too apt to begin their Declarations with
saying, that God is offended when People differ
from them in Opinion; in which they too much
resemble the bad Poets, who us'd to declare
publickly that *Boileau* spake irreverently of
Lewis the Fourteenth, because he ridicul'd their
stupid Productions. Bishop *Stillingfleet* got the
Reputation of a calm and unprejudic'd Divine,
because he did not expressly make use of in-
jurious Terms in his Dispute with Mr. *Locke*.
That Divine entred the Lists against him, but
was defeated; for he argued as a Schoolman,

and *Locke* as a Philosopher, who was perfectly acquainted with the strong as well as the weak Side of the human Mind, and who fought with Weapons whose Temper he knew. If I might presume to give my Opinion on so delicate a Subject after Mr. *Locke*, I would say, that Men have long disputed on the Nature and the Immortality of the Soul. With regard to its Immortality, 'tis impossible to give a Demonstration of it, since its Nature is still the Subject of Controversy; which however must be thoroughly understood, before a Person can be able to determine whether it be immortal or not. Human reason is so little able, merely by its own Strength, to demonstrate the Immortality of the Soul, that 'twas absolutely necessary Religion should reveal it to us. 'Tis of Advantage to Society in general, that Mankind should believe the Soul to be immortal; Faith commands us to do this; nothing more is requir'd, and the Matter is clear'd up at once. But 'tis otherwise with respect to its Nature; 'tis of little Importance to Religion, which only requires the Soul to be virtuous, what Substance it may be made of. 'Tis a Clock which is given us to regulate, but the Artist has not told us what Materials the Spring of this Clock is compos'd.

I am a Body and, I think, that's all I know of the Matter. Shall I ascribe to an unknown Cause, I can so easily impute to the only second Cause I am acquainted with? Here all the School Philosophers interrupt me with their Arguments, and declare that there is only Extension and Solidity in Bodies, and that there they can have nothing but Motion and Figure. Now Motion, Figure, Extension and Solidity cannot form a Thought, and consequently the Soul cannot be Matter. All this, so often repeated, mighty Series of Reasoning, amounts to no more than this; I am absolutely ignorant what Matter is; I guess but imperfectly, some Properties of it; now, I absolutely cannot tell whether these Properties may be joyn'd to Thought. As I therefore know nothing, I maintain positively that Matter cannot think. In this Manner do the Schools reason.

Mr. *Locke* address'd these Gentlemen in the candid, sincere Manner following. At least confess your selves to be as ignorant as I. Neither your Imaginations nor mine are able to comprehend in what manner a Body is susceptible of Ideas; and do you conceive better in what manner a Substance, of what kind soever, is susceptible of them? As you cannot comprehend either Matter or Spirit, why will you presume to assert any thing?

The superstitious Man comes afterwards, and declares, that all those must be burnt for the Good of their Souls, who so much as suspect that 'tis possible for the Body to think without any foreign Assistance. But what would these People say should they themselves be prov'd irreligious? And indeed, what Man can presume to assert, without being guilty at the same time of the greatest Impiety, that 'tis impossible for the Creator to form Matter with Thought and Sensation? Consider only, I beg you, what a Dilemma you bring yourselves into; you who confine in this Manner the Power of the Creator. Beasts have the same Organs, the same Sensations, the same Perceptions as we; they have Memory, and combine certain Ideas. In case it was not in the Power of God to animate Matter, and inform it with Sensation, the Consequence would be, either that Beasts are mere Machines, or that they have a spiritual Soul.

METHINKS 'tis clearly evident that Beasts cannot be mere Machines, which I prove thus. God has given them the very same Organs of Sensation as to us: If therefore they have no Sensation, God has created a useless Thing; now according to your own Confession God does nothing in vain; he therefore did not create so many Organs of Sensation, merely for them to be uninform'd with this Faculty; consequently Beasts are not mere Machines. Beasts, according to your Assertion, cannot be animated with a spiritual Soul; you will therefore, in spight of your self, be reduc'd to this only Assertion, *viz.* that God has endued the Organs of Beasts, who are mere Matter, with the Faculties of Sensation and Perception, which you call Instinct in them. But why may not God if he pleases, communicate to our more delicate Organs, that Faculty of feeling, perceiving, and thinking, which we call human Reason? To whatever Side you turn, you are forc'd to acknowledge your own Ignorance, and the boundless Power of the Creator. Exclaim therefore no more against the sage, the modest Philosophy of Mr. *Locke*, which so far from interfering with Religion, would be of use to demonstrate the Truth of it, in case Religion wanted any such Support. For what Philosophy can be of a more religious Nature than that, which affirming nothing but what it conceives clearly; and conscious of its own Weakness, declares that we must always have recourse to God in our examining of the first Principles.

BESIDES, we must not be apprehensive, that any philosophical Opinion will ever prejudice the Religion of a Country. Tho' our Demonstrations clash directly with our Mysteries, that's nothing to the Purpose, for the latter are not less rever'd upon that Account by our Christian Philosophers, who know very well that the Objects of Reason and those of Faith are of a very different Nature. Philosophers will never form a religious Sect, the Reason of which is, their Writings are not calculated for the Vulgar, and they themselves are free from Enthusiasm. If we divide Mankind into twenty Parts, 'twill be found that nineteen of these consist of Persons employ'd in manual Labour, who will never know that such a Man as Mr. *Locke* existed. In the remaining twentieth Part how few are Readers? And among such as are so, twenty amuse themselves with Romances to one who studies Philosophy. The thinking Part of Mankind are confin'd to a very small Number, and these will never disturb the Peace and Tranquillity of the World.

NEITHER *Montagne, Locke, Bayle, Spinoza, Hobbes*, the Lord *Shaftsbury, Collins* nor *Toland* lighted up the Firebrand of Discord in their Countries; this has generally been the Work of Divines, who being at first puff'd up with the Ambition of becoming Chiefs of a Sect, soon grew very desirous of being at the Head of a Party. But what do I say? All the Works of the modern Philosophers put together will never make so much Noise as even the Dispute which arose among the *Franciscans*, merely about the Fashion of their Sleeves and of their Cowls.

LETTER XIV.

ON

DES CARTES

AND

Sir ISAAC NEWTON.

A FRENCHMAN who arrives in *London*, will find Philosophy, like every Thing else, very much chang'd there. He had left the World a *plenum*, and he now finds it a *vacuum*. At *Paris* the Universe is seen, compos'd of Vortices of subtile Matter; but nothing like it is seen in *London*. In *France*, 'tis the Pressure of the Moon that causes the Tides; but in *England* 'tis the Sea that gravitates towards the Moon; so that when you think that the Moon should make it Flood with us, those Gentlemen fancy it should be Ebb, which, very unluckily, cannot be prov'd. For to be able to do this, 'tis necessary the Moon and the Tides should have been enquir'd into, at the very instant of the Creation.

Y O U ' L L observe farther, that the Sun, which in *France* is said to have nothing to do in the Affair, comes in here for very near a quarter of its Assistance. According to your *Cartesians*, every Thing is perform'd by an Impulsion, of which we have very little Notion; and according to Sir *Isaac Newton*, 'tis by an Attraction, the Cause of which is as much unknown to us. At *Paris* you imagine that the Earth is shap'd like a Melon, or of an oblique Figure; at *London* it has an oblate one. A *Cartesian* declares that Light exists in the Air; but a *Newtonian* asserts that it comes from the Sun in six Minutes and a half. The several Operations of your Chymistry are perform'd by Acids, Alkalies and subtile Matter; but Attraction prevails even in Chymistry among the *English*.

T H E very Essence of Things is totally chang'd. You neither are agreed upon the Definition of the Soul, nor on that of Matter. *Descartes*, as I observ'd in my last, maintains that the Soul is the same Thing with Thought, and Mr. *Locke* has given a pretty good Proof of the contrary.

D E S C A R T E S asserts farther, that Extension alone constitutes Matter, but Sir *Isaac* adds Solidity to it.

H o w furiously contradictory are these Opinions!

Non nostrum inter vos tantas componere lites.
　　　　　　　Virgil, Eclog. III.

　'Tis not for us to end such great Disputes.

This famous *Newton*, this Destroyer of the *Cartesian* System, died in *March Anno* 1727. His Countrymen honour'd him in his Life-Time, and interr'd him as tho' he had been a King who had made his People happy.

T h e *English* read with the highest Satisfaction, and translated into their Tongue, the Elogium of Sir *Isaac Newton*, which Mr. *de Fontenelle* spoke in the Academy of Sciences. Mr. *de Fontenelle* presides as Judge over Philosophers; and the *English* expected his Decision, as a solemn Declaration of the Superiority of the *English* Philosophy over that of the *French*. But when 'twas found that this Gentleman had compar'd *Des Cartes* to Sir *Isaac*, the whole Royal Society in *London* rose up in Arms. So far from acquiescing with Mr. *Fontenelle's* Judgment, they criticis'd his Discourse. And even several (who however were not the ablest Philosophers in that Body) were offended at the Comparison; and for no other Reason but because *Des Cartes* was a *Frenchman.*

I t must be confess'd that these two great Men differ'd very much in Conduct, in Fortune, and in Philosophy.

N a t u r e had indulg'd *Des Cartes* a shining and strong Imagination, whence he became a

very singular Person both in private Life, and
in his Manner of Reasoning. This Imagination
could not conceal it self even in his philosophical
Works, which are every where adorn'd with
very shining, ingenious Metaphors and Figures.
Nature had almost made him a Poet; and indeed he
wrote a Piece of Poetry for the Entertainment of
Christina Queen of *Sweden*, which however was
suppress'd in Honour to his Memory.

HE embrac'd a Military Life for some Time,
and afterwards becoming a complete Philosopher,
he did not think the Passion of Love derogatory
to his Character. He had by his Mistress a
Daughter call'd *Froncine*, who died young, and
was very much regretted by him. Thus he experienc'd every Passion incident to Mankind.

HE was a long Time of Opinion, that it would
be necessary for him to fly from the Society of
his Fellow Creatures, and especially from his
native Country, in order to enjoy the Happiness
of cultivating his philosophical Studies in full
Liberty.

DES CARTES was very right, for his Cotemporaries were not knowing enough to improve and enlighten his Understanding, and
were capable of little else than of giving him
Uneasiness.

He left *France* purely to go in search of Truth,
which was then persecuted by the wretched
Philosophy of the Schools. However, he found
that Reason was as much disguis'd and deprav'd

in the Universities of *Holland*, into which he
withdrew, as in his own Country. For at the
Time that the *French* condemn'd the only Pro-
positions of his Philosophy which were true, he
was persectued by the pretended Philosophers
of *Holland*, who understood him no better; and
who, having a nearer View of his Glory, hated
his Person the more, so that he was oblig'd to
leave *Utrecht*. *Des Cartes* was injuriously accus'd
of being an Atheist, the last Refuge of religious
Scandal: And he who had employ'd all the
Sagacity and Penetration of his Genius, in
searching for new Proofs of the Existence of a
God, was suspected to believe there was no
such Being.

SUCH a Persecution from all Sides, must
necessarily suppose a most exalted Merit as well
as a very distinguish'd Reputation, and indeed he
possess'd both. Reason at that Time darted a Ray
upon the World thro' the Gloom of the Schools,
and the Prejudices of popular Superstition.
At last his Name spread so universally, that the
French were desirous of bringing him back into
his native Country by Rewards, and accordingly
offer'd him an annual Pension of a thousand
Crowns. Upon these Hopes *Des Cartes* return'd
to *France*; paid the Fees of his Patent, which
was sold at that Time, but no Pension was settled
upon him. Thus disappointed, he return'd to
his Solitude in *North-Holland*, where he again
pursued the Study of Philosophy, whilst the

great *Galileo*, at fourscore Years of Age, was groaning in the Prisons of the Inquisition, only for having demonstrated the Earth's Motion.

A T last *Des Cartes* was snatch'd from the World in the Flower of his Age at *Stockholm*. His Death was owing to a bad Regimen, and he expir'd in the Midst of some *Literati* who were his Enemies, and under the Hands of a Physician to whom he was odious.

T H E Progress of Sir *Isaac Newton's* Life was quite different. He liv'd happy, and very much honour'd in his native Country, to the Age of fourscore and five Years.

'T w a s his peculiar Felicity, not only to be born in a Country of Liberty, but in an Age when all scholastic Impertinencies were banish'd from the World. Reason alone was cultivated, and Mankind cou'd only be his Pupil, not his Enemy.

O n e very singular Difference in the Lives of these two great Men is, that Sir *Isaac*, during the long Course of Years he enjoy'd, was never sensible to any Passion, was not subject to the common Frailties of Mankind, nor ever had any Commerce with Women; a Circumstance which was assur'd me by the Physician and Surgeon who attended him in his last Moments.

W e may admire Sir *Isaac Newton* on this Occasion, but then we must not censure *Des Cartes*.

T h e Opinion that generally prevails in *England* with regard to these two Philosophers is, that the latter was a Dreamer, and the former a Sage.

VERY few People in *England* read *Descartes*, whose Works indeed are now useless. On the other Side, but a small Number peruse those of Sir *Isaac*, because to do this the Student must be deeply skill'd in the Mathematicks, otherwise those Works will be unintelligible to him. But notwithstanding this, these great Men are the Subject of every One's Discourse. Sir *Isaac Newton* is allow'd every Advantage, whilst *Des Cartes* is not indulg'd a single one. According to some, 'tis to the former that we owe the Discovery of a *Vacuum*, that the Air is a heavy Body, and the Invention of Telescopes. In a Word, Sir *Isaac Newton* is here as the *Hercules* of fabulous Story, to whom the Ignorant ascrib'd all the Feats of ancient Heroes.

IN a Critique that was made in *London* on Mr. *de Fontenelle's* Discourse, the Writer presum'd to assert that *Des Cartes* was not a great Geometrician. Those who make such a Declaration may justly be reproach'd with flying in in their Master's Face. *Des Cartes* extended the Limits of Geometry as far beyond the Place where he found them, as Sir *Isaac* did after him. The former first taught the Method of expressing Curves by Equations. This Geometry which, Thanks to him for it, is now grown common, was so abstruse in his Time, that not so much as one Professor would undertake to explain it; and *Schotten* in *Holland*, and *Format* in *France*, were the only Men who understood it.

HE applied this geometrical and inventive Genius to Dioptricks, which, when treated of by him, became a new Art. And if he was mistaken in some Things, the Reason of that is, a Man who discovers a new Tract of Land cannot at once know all the Properties of the Soil. Those who come after him, and make these Lands fruitful, are at least oblig'd to him for the Discovery. I will not deny but that there are innumerable Errors in the rest of *Des Cartes's* Works.

GEOMETRY was a Guide he himself had in some Measure fashion'd, which would have conducted him safely thro' the several Paths of natural Philosophy. Nevertheless he at last abandon'd this Guide, and gave entirely into the Humour of forming Hypotheses; and then Philosophy was no more than an ingenious Romance, fit only to amuse the Ignorant. He was mistaken in the Nature of the Soul, in the Proofs of the Existence of a God, in Matter, in the Laws of Motion, and in the Nature of Light. He admitted innate Ideas, he invented new Elements, he created a World; he made Man according to his own Fancy; and 'tis justly said, that the Man of *Des Cartes* is in Fact that of *Des Cartes* only, very different from the real one.

HE push'd his metaphysical Errors so far, as to declare that two and two make four, for no other Reason but because God would have it so. However, 'twill not be making him too great a Compliment if we affirm that he was valuable even in his Mistakes. He deceiv'd himself, but then it was at least in a methodical Way. He destroy'd all the absurd Chimæra's with which Youth had been infatuated for two thousand Years. He taught his Cotemporaries how to reason, and enabled them to employ his own Weapons against himself. If *Des Cartes* did not pay in good Money, he however did great Service in crying down that of a base Alloy.

I INDEED believe, that very few will presume to compare his Philosophy in any respect with that of Sir *Isaac Newton*. The former is an Essay, the latter a Master-Piece: But then the Man who first brought us to the Path of Truth, was perhaps as great a Genius as he who afterwards conducted us through it.

DES CARTES gave Sight to the Blind. These saw the Errors of Antiquity and of the Sciences. The Path he struck out is since become boundless. *Rohault's* little Work was during some Years a complete System of Physicks; but now all the Transactions of the several Academies in *Europe* put together do not form so much as the Beginning of a System. In fathoming this Abyss no Bottom has been found. We are now to examine what Discoveries Sir *Isaac Newton* has made in it.

LETTER XV.

ON

ATTRACTION.

THE Discoveries which gain'd Sir *Isaac Newton* so universal a Reputation, relate to the System of the World, to Light, to Geometrical Infinites; and lastly to Chronology, with which he us'd to amuse himself after the Fatigue of his severer Studies.

I WILL now acquaint you (without Prolixity if possible) with the few Things I have been able to comprehend of all these sublime Ideas. With Regard to the System of our World, Disputes were a long Time maintain'd, on the Cause that turns the Planets, and keeps them in their Orbits; and on those Causes which make all Bodies here below descend towards the Surface of the Earth.

THE System of *Des Cartes* explain'd and improv'd since his Time, seem'd to give a plausible Reason for all those Phænomena; and this Reason seem'd more just, as 'tis simple, and intelligible to all Capacities. But in Philosophy, a Student ought to doubt of the Things he fancies he understands too easily, as much as of those he does not understand.

GRAVITY, the falling of accelerated Bodies on the Earth, the Revolution of the Planets in their Orbits, their Rotations round their Axis, all this is mere Motion. Now Motion can't perhaps be conceiv'd any otherwise than by Impulsion; therefore all those Bodies must be impelled. But by what are they impelled? All Space is full, it therefore is fill'd with a very subtile Matter, since this is imperceptible to us; this Matter goes from West to East, since all the Planets are carried from West to East. Thus from Hypothesis to Hypothesis, from one Appearance to another, Philosophers have imagin'd a vast Whirlpool of subtile Matter, in which the Planets are carried round the Sun: They also have created another particular Vortex which floats in the great one, and which turns daily round the Planets. When all this is done, 'tis pretended that Gravity depends on this diurnal Motion; for, say these, the Velocity of the subtile Matter that turns round our little Vortex, must be seventeen Times more rapid than that of the Earth; or, in case its Velocity is seventeen Times greater than that of the Earth, its centrifugal Force must be vastly greater, and consequently impell all Bodies towards the Earth. This is the Cause of Gravity, according to the *Cartesian* System. But the Theorist, before he calculated the centrifugal Force and Velocity of the subtile Matter, should first have been certain that it existed.

S I R *Isaac Newton* seems to have destroy'd all these great and little Vortices, both that which carries the Planets round the Sun, as well as the other which supposes every Planet to turn on its own Axis.

F I R S T, with regard to the pretended little Vortex of the Earth, 'tis demonstrated that it must lose its Motion by insensible Degrees; 'tis demonstrated, that if the Earth swims in a Fluid, its Density must be equal to that of the Earth; and in case its Density be the same, all the Bodies we endeavour to move must meet with an insuperable Resistance.

W I T H regard to the great Vortices, they are still more chimerical, and 'tis impossible to make them agree with *Kepler's* Law, the Truth of which has been demonstrated. Sir *Isaac* shows, that the Revolution of the Fluid in which *Jupiter* is suppos'd to be carried, is not the same with regard to the Revolution of the Fluid of the Earth, as the Revolution of *Jupiter* with respect to that of the Earth. He proves, that as the Planets make their Revolutions in Elipsis's, and consequently being at a much greater Distance one from the other in their *Aphelia*, and a little nearer in their *Perihelia*; the Earth's Velocity, for Instance, ought to be greater, when 'tis nearer *Venus* and *Mars*, because the Fluid that carries it along, being then more press'd, ought to have a greater Motion; and yet 'tis even then that the Earth's Motion is slower.

HE proves that there is no such Thing as a celestial Matter which goes from West to East, since the Comets traverse those Spaces, sometimes from East to West, and at other Times from North to South.

IN fine, the better to resolve, if possible, every Difficulty, he proves, and even by Experiments, that 'tis impossible there should be a *Plenum*; and brings back the *Vacuum*, which *Aristotle* and *Des Cartes* had banish'd from the World.

HAVING by these and several other Arguments destroy'd the *Cartesian* Vortices, he despair'd of ever being able to discover, whether there is a secret Principle in Nature which, at the same Time, is the Cause of the Motion of all celestial Bodies, and that of Gravity on the Earth. But being retir'd in 1666, upon Account of the Plague, to a Solitude near *Cambridge*; as he was walking one Day in his Garden, and saw some Fruits fall from a Tree, he fell into a profound Meditation on that Gravity, the Cause of which had so long been sought, but in vain, by all the Philosophers, whilst the Vulgar think there is nothing mysterious in it. He said to himself, that from what height soever, in our Hemisphere, those Bodies might descend, their

Fall wou'd certainly be in the Progression dis-cover'd by *Galileo*; and the Spaces they run thro' would be as the Square of the Times. Why may not this Power which causes heavy Bodies to descend, and is the same without any sensible Diminution at the remotest Distance from the Center of the Earth, or on the Sum-mits of the highest Mountains; Why, said Sir *Isaac*, may not this Power extend as high as the Moon? And in Case, its Influence reaches so far, is it not very probable that this Power re-tains it in its Orbit, and determines its Motion? But in case the Moon obeys this Principle (whatever it be) may we not conclude very naturally, that the rest of the Planets are equally subject to it? In case this Power exists (which besides is prov'd) it must increase in an inverse *Ratio* of the Squares of the Distances. All there-fore that remains is, to examine how far a heavy Body, which should fall upon the Earth from a moderate height, would go; and how far in the same time, a Body which should fall from the Orbit of the Moon, would descend. To find this, nothing is wanted but the Measure of the Earth, and the Distance of the Moon from it.

THUS Sir *Isaac Newton* reason'd. But at that Time the *English* had but a very imperfect Measure of our Globe, and depended on the uncertain Supposition of Mariners, who com-puted a Degree to contain but sixty *English* Miles, whereas it consists in reality of near

H

seventy. As this false Computation did not agree with the Conclusions which Sir *Isaac* intended to draw from them, he laid aside this Pursuit. A half-learn'd Philosopher, remarkable only for his Vanity, would have made the Measure of the Earth agree, any how, with his System: Sir *Isaac*, however, chose rather to quit the Researches he was then engag'd in. But after Mr. *Picart* had measur'd the Earth exactly, by tracing that Meridian, which redounds so much to the Honour of the *French*, Sir *Isaac Newton* resum'd his former Reflexions, and found his Account in Mr. *Picart's* Calculation.

A CIRCUMSTANCE which has always appear'd wonderful to me, is, that such sublime Discoveries should have been made by the sole Assistance of a Quadrant and a little Arithmetic.

THE Circumference of the Earth is one hundred twenty three Millions, two hundred forty nine thousand six hundred Feet. This, among other Things, is necessary to prove the System of Attraction.

THE instant we know the Earth's Circumference, and the Distance of the Moon, we know that of the Moon's Orbit, and the Diameter of this Orbit. The Moon performs its Revolution in that Orbit in twenty seven Days, seven Hours, forty three Minutes. 'Tis demonstrated, that the Moon in its mean Motion makes an hundred and fourscore and seven thousand, nine hundred and sixty Feet (of *Paris*) in a Minute. 'Tis likewise demonstrated, by a known Theorem, that the central Force which should make a Body fall from the height of the Moon, would make its Velocity no more than fifteen *Paris* Feet in a Minute of Time. Now, if the Law by which Bodies gravitate, and attract one another in an inverse Ratio of the Squares of the Distances be true; if the same Power acts, according to that Law, throughout all Nature; 'tis evident that as the Earth is sixty Semi-diameters distant from the Moon, a heavy Body must necessarily fall (on the Earth) fifteen Feet in the first Second, and fifty four thousand Feet in the first Minute.

N o w a heavy Body falls, in reality, fifteen Feet in the first Second, and goes in the first Minute fifty four thousand Foot, which Number is the Square of sixty multiplied by fifteen. Bodies therefore gravitate in an inverse Ratio of the Squares of the Distances; consequently, what causes Gravity on Earth, and keeps the Moon in its Orbit, is one and the same Power; it being demonstrated that the Moon gravitates on the Earth, which is the Center of its particular Motion, 'tis demonstrated that the Earth and the Moon gravitate on the Sun which is the Center of their annual Motion.

T h e rest of the Planets must be subject to this general Law; and if this Law exists, these Planets must follow the Laws which *Kepler* discover'd. All these Laws, all these Relations are indeed observ'd by the Planets with the utmost Exactness; therefore the Power of Attraction causes all the Planets to gravitate towards the Sun, in like Manner as the Moon gravitates towards our Globe.

FINALLY, as in all Bodies, Re-action is equal to Action, 'tis certain that the Earth gravitates also towards the Moon; and that the Sun gravitates towards both: That every one of the Satellites of *Saturn* gravitates towards the other four, and the other four towards it: All five towards *Saturn*, and *Saturn* towards all. That 'tis the same with regard to *Jupiter*; and that all these Globes are attracted by the Sun, which is reciprocally attracted by them.

THIS Power of Gravitation acts proportionately to the Quantity of Matter in Bodies, a Truth which Sir *Isaac* has demonstrated by Experiments. This new Discovery has been of use to show, that the Sun (the Center of the planetary System) attracts them all in a direct Ratio of their Quantity of Matter combin'd with their Nearness. From hence Sir *Isaac*, rising by Degrees to Discoveries which seem'd not to be form'd for the human Mind, is bold enough to compute the Quantity of Matter contain'd in the Sun and in every Planet; and in this Manner shows, from the simple Laws of Mechanicks, that every celestial Globe ought necessarily to be where it is plac'd.

HIS bare Principle of the Laws of Gravitation, accounts for all the apparent Inequalities

in the Course of the celestial Globes. The Varia-
tions of the Moon are a necessary Consequence
of those Laws. Moreover, the Reason is evidently
seen why the Nodes of the Moon perform their
Revolutions in nineteen Years, and those of
the Earth in about twenty six Thousand. The
several Appearances observ'd in the Tides, are
also a very simple Effect of this Attraction. The
Proximity of the Moon when at the full, and
when it is new, and its Distance in the Quadra-
tures or Quarters combin'd with the Action of
the Sun, exhibit a sensible Reason why the
Ocean swells and sinks.

A F T E R having shown, by his sublime Theory,
the Course and Inequalities of the Planets, he
subjects Comets to the same Law. The Orbit
of these Fires (unknown for so great a Series of
Years,) which was the Terror of Mankind, and
the Rock against which Philosophy split; plac'd
by *Aristotle* below the Moon, and sent back by
Des Cartes above the Sphere of *Saturn*, is at
last plac'd in its proper Seat by Sir *Isaac Newton*.

H E proves that Comets are solid Bodies
which move in the Sphere of the Sun's Activity;
and that they describe an Ellipsis so very eccen-
tric, and so near to Parabola's, that certain
Comets must take up above five hundred Years
in their Revolution.

T H E learned Dr. *Halley* is of opinion, that
the Comet seen in 1680, is the same which appear'd in *Julius Cæsar's* Time. This shows more

than any other, that Comets are hard, opake
Bodies; for it descended so near to the Sun, as
to come within a sixth Part of the Diameter of
this Planet from it; and consequently might
have contracted a Degree of Heat two thousand
Times stronger than that of red hot Iron; and
would have been soon dispers'd in Vapour, had
it not been a firm, dense Body. The guessing
the Course of Comets began then to be very
much in vogue: The celebrated *Bernoulli* concluded by his System, that the famous Comet
of 1680, would appear again the 17th of *May*
1719. Not a single Astronomer in *Europe* went
to Bed that Night; however they needed not to
have broke their Rest, for the famous Comet
never appear'd. There is at least more Cun-
ning, if not more Certainty, in fixing its Return
to so remote a Distance as five hundred and
seventy five Years. As to Mr. *Whiston*, he
affirm'd very seriously, that in the Time of the
Deluge a Comet overflow'd the terrestrial Globe;
and he was so unreasonable as to wonder that
People laugh'd at him for making such an Assertion. The Ancients were almost in the same way
of Thinking with Mr. *Whiston*, and fancied that
Comets were always the Fore-runners of some
great Calamity which was to befall Mankind.
Sir *Isaac Newton*, on the contrary, suspected
that they are very beneficent; and that Vapours
exhale from them merely to nourish and vivify
the Planets, which imbibe in their Course the

several Particles the Sun has detach'd from the Comets; an Opinion which at least is more probable than the former. But this is not all. If this Power of Gravitation or Attraction acts on all the celestial Globes, it acts undoubtedly on the several Parts of these Globes. For in case Bodies attract one another in Proportion to the Quantity of Matter contain'd in them, it can only be in Proportion to the Quantity of their Parts; and if this Power is found in the whole, 'tis undoubtedly in the half, in the quarter, in the eighth Part, and so on in *infinitum*.

THIS is Attraction, the great Spring by which all Nature is mov'd. Sir *Isaac Newton* after having demonstrated the Existence of this Principle, plainly foresaw that its very Name wou'd offend; and therefore this Philosopher in more Places than one of his Books, gives the Reader some Caution about it. He bids him beware of confounding this Name with what the Ancients call'd occult Qualities; but to be satisfied with knowing that there is in all Bodies a central Force which acts to the utmost Limits of the Universe, according to the invariable Laws of Mechanicks.

'T I S surprising, after the solemn Protestations Sir *Isaac* made, that such eminent Men as Mr. *Sorin* and Mr. *de Fontenelle*, should have imputed to this great Philosopher the verbal and chimerical Way of Reasoning of the *Aristoteleans*; Mr. *Sorin* in the Memoirs of the Academy of

1709, and Mr. *de Fontenelle* in the very Elogium of Sir *Isaac Newton*.

MOST of the *French*, the Learned and others, have repeated this Reproach. These are for ever crying out, why did he not imploy the Word *Impulsion*, which is so well understood, rather than that of *Attraction*, which is unintelligible.

SIR *Isaac* might have answer'd these Criticks thus: First, you have as imperfect an Idea of the Word Impulsion, as that of Attraction; and in case you cannot conceive how one Body tends towards the Center of another Body, neither can you conceive by what Power one Body can impell another.

SECONDLY, I cou'd not admit of Impulsion, for to do this, I must have known that a celestial Matter was the Agent; but so far from knowing that there is any such Matter, I have prov'd it to be merely imaginary.

THIRDLY, I use the Word Attraction for no other Reason, but to express an Effect which I discover'd in Nature; a certain and indisputable Effect of an unknown Principle; a Quality inherent in Matter, the Cause of which Persons of greater Abilities than I can pretend to, may, if they can, find out.

WHAT have you then taught us? Will these People say further: And to what Purpose are so many Calculations to tell us what you yourself don't comprehend?

I HAVE taught you, may Sir *Isaac* rejoin,

that all Bodies gravitate towards one another in proportion to their Quantity of Matter; that these central Forces alone, keep the Planets and Comets in their Orbits, and cause them to move in the Proportion before set down. I demonstrate to you, that 'tis impossible there should be any other Cause which keeps the Planets in their Orbits, than that general Phenomenon of Gravity. For heavy Bodies fall on the Earth according to the Proportion demonstrated of central Forces; and the Planets finishing their Course according to these same Proportions, in case there were another Power that acted upon all those Bodies, it would either increase their Velocity, or change their Direction. Now not one of those Bodies ever has a single Degree of Motion or Velocity, or has any Direction but what is demonstrated to be the Effect of the central Forces; consequently 'tis impossible there should be any other Principle.

G I V E me Leave once more to introduce Sir *Isaac* speaking: Shall he not be allow'd to say, My Case and that of the Ancients is very different. These saw, for Instance, Water ascend in Pumps, and said, the Water rises because it abhors a *Vacuum*. But with regard to my self, I am in the Case of a Man who should have first observ'd that Water ascends in Pumps, but should leave others to explain the Cause of this Effect. The Anatomist who first declar'd, that the Motion of the Arm is owing to the

Contraction of the Muscles, taught Mankind an indisputable Truth; but are they less oblig'd to him because he did not know the Reason why the Muscles contract? The Cause of the Elasticity of the Air is unknown, but he who first discover'd this Spring perform'd a very signal Service to natural Philosophy. The Spring that I discover'd was more hidden and more universal, and for that very Reason Mankind ought to thank me the more. I have discover'd a new Property of Matter, one of the Secrets of the Creator; and have calculated and discover'd the Effects of it. After this shall People quarrel with me about the Name I give it.

VORTICES may be call'd an occult Quality because their Existence was never prov'd: Attraction on the contrary is a real Thing, because its Effects are demonstrated, and the Proportions of it are calculated. The Cause of this Cause is among the *Arcana* of the Almighty.

Procedes huc, & non amplius.
Hither thou shalt go, and no farther.

LETTER XVI.

ON

Sir *Isaac Newton*'s

OPTICKS.

THE Philosophers of the last Age found out a new Universe; and a Circumstance which made its Discovery more difficult, was, that no one had so much as suspected its Existence. The most Sage and Judicious were of Opinion, that 'twas a frantic Rashness to dare so much as to imagine that it was possible to guess the Laws by which the celestial Bodies move, and the manner how Light acts. *Galileo* by his astronomical Discoveries, *Kepler* by his *Calculation, Des Cartes* (at least in his Dioptricks), and Sir *Isaac Newton* in all his Works, severally saw the Mechanism of the Springs of the World. The Geometricians have subjected Infinity to the Laws of Calculation. The Circulation of the Blood in Animals, and of the Sap in Vegetables, have chang'd the Face of Nature with regard to us. A new kind of Existence has been given to Bodies in the Air-Pump. By the Assistance of Telescopes Bodies have been brought nearer to one another. Finally, the several Discoveries which Sir *Isaac Newton* has made on Light, are equal to the boldest Things which the Curiosity of Man could expect, after so many philosophical Novelties.

TILL *Antonio de Dominis*, the Rainbow was consider'd as an inexplicable Miracle. This Philosopher guess'd that it was a necessary Effect of the Sun and Rain. *Des Cartes* gain'd immortal Fame, by his mathematical Explication of this so natural a Phænomenon. He calculated the Reflexions and Refractions of Light in Drops of Rain; and his Sagacity on this Occasion was at that Time look'd upon as next to divine.

BUT what would he have said had it been prov'd to him that he was mistaken in the Nature of Light; that he had not the least Reason to maintain that 'tis a globular Body: That 'tis false to assert, that this Matter spreading it self through the whole, waits only to be projected forward by the Sun, in order to be put in Action, in like Manner as a long Staff acts at one end when push'd forward by the other? That Light is certainly darted by the Sun; in fine, that Light is transmitted from the Sun to the Earth in about seven Minutes, tho' a Cannon Ball, which

were not to lose any of its Velocity, cou'd not go
that Distance in less than twenty five Years?
How great wou'd have been his Astonishment,
had he been told, that Light does not reflect
directly by impinging against the solid Parts of
Bodies; that Bodies are not transparent when
they have large Pores; and that a Man should
arise, who would demonstrate all these Para-
doxes, and anatomize a single Ray of Light with
more Dexterity than the ablest Artist dissects a
human Body. This Man is come. Sir *Isaac
Newton* has demonstrated to the Eye, by the
bare Assistance of the Prism, that Light is a
Composition of colour'd Rays, which, being
united, form the white Colour. A single Ray is
by him divided into seven, which all fall upon
a Piece of Linen, or a Sheet of white Paper, in
their Order one above the other, and at unequal
Distances. The first is Red, the second Orange,
the third Yellow, the fourth Green, the fifth
Blue, the sixth Indigo, the seventh a Violet
Purple. Each of these Rays transmitted afterwards by an hundred other Prisms, will never
change the Colour it bears; in like Manner as
Gold, when completely purg'd from its Dross,
will never change afterwards in the Crucible.
As a superabundant Proof that each of these
elementary Rays has inherently in it self that
which forms its Colour to the Eye, take a small
Piece of yellow Wood for Instance, and set it
in the Ray of a red Colour, this Wood will

instantly be ting'd red; but set it in the Ray of
a green Colour, it assumes a green Colour, and
so of all the rest.

FROM what Cause therefore do Colours
arise in Nature? 'Tis nothing but the Disposition of Bodies to reflect the Rays of a certain
Order, and to absorb all the rest.

WHAT then is this secret Disposition? Sir
Isaac Newton demonstrates, that 'tis nothing
more than the Density of the small constituent
Particles of which a Body is compos'd. And how
is this Reflexion perform'd? 'Twas suppos'd to
arise from the Rebounding of the Rays, in the
same Manner as a Ball on the Surface of a solid
Body; but this is a Mistake, for Sir *Isaac* taught
the astonish'd Philosophers, that Bodies are
opake for no other Reason, but because their
Pores are large; that Light reflects on our Eyes
from the very Bosom of those Pores; that the
smaller the Pores of a Body are, the more such a
Body is transparent. Thus Paper which reflects
the Light when dry, transmits it when oil'd,
because the Oil, by filling its Pores, makes them
much smaller.

'TIS there that examining the vast Porosity
of Bodies, every Particle having its Pores, and
every Particle of those Particles having its own;
he shows we are not certain that there is a cubic
Inch of solid Matter in the Universe, so far are
we from conceiving what Matter is. Having thus
divided, as it were, Light into its Elements, and

carried the Sagacity of his Discoveries so far, as to prove the Method of distinguishing compound Colours from such as are primitive; he shews, that these elementary Rays separated by the Prism, are rang'd in their Order for no other Reason but because they are refracted in that very Order; and 'tis this Property (unknown till he discover'd it) of breaking or splitting in this Proportion; 'tis this unequal Refraction of Rays, this Power of refracting the red less than the orange Colour, &c. which he calls the different Refrangibility. The most reflexible Rays are the most refrangible, and from hence he evinces that the same Power is the Cause both of the Reflection and Refraction of Light.

B U T all these Wonders are merely but the Opening of his Discoveries. He found out the Secret to see the Vibrations or Fits of Light, which come and go incessantly, and which either transmit Light or reflect it according to the Density of the Parts they meet with. He has presum'd to calculate the Density of the Particles of Air necessary between two Glasses, the one flat, the other convex on one side, set one upon the other; in order to operate such a Transmission or Reflexion, or to form such and such a Colour.

F R O M all these Combinations he discovers the Proportion in which Light acts on Bodies, and Bodies act on Light.

H E saw Light so perfectly, that he has de-
termin'd to what Degree of Perfection the Art
of increasing it, and of assisting our Eyes by
Telescopes can be carried.

D E S C A R T E S, from a noble Confidence,
that was very excusable considering how strongly
he was fir'd at the first Discoveries he made in
an Art which he almost first found out; *Des
Cartes*, I say, hop'd to discover in the Stars, by
the Assistance of Telescopes, Objects as small
as those we discern upon the Earth.

B U T Sir *Isaac* has shown, that Dioptric
Telescopes cannot be brought to a greater Perfection; because of that Refraction, and of that
very Refrangibility, which at the same Time
that they bring Objects nearer to us, scatter too
much the elementary Rays; he has calculated
in these Glasses the Proportion of the scatter-
ing of the red and of the blue Rays; and pro-
ceeding so far as to demonstrate Things which
were not suppos'd even to exist, he examines
the Inequalities which arise from the Shape or
Figure of the Glass, and that which arises from
the Refrangibility. He finds, that the object
Glass of the Telescope being convex on one
side and flat on the other, in case the flat Side
be turn'd towards the Object, the Error which
arises from the Construction and Position of
the Glass, is above five thousand Times less
than the Error which arises from the Refrangibility: And therefore, that the Shape or Figure

of the Glasses is not the Cause why Telescopes cannot be carried to a greater Perfection, but arises wholly from the Nature of Light.

F o r this Reason he invented a Telescope, which discovers Objects by Reflection and not by Refraction. Telescopes of this new kind are very hard to make, and their Use is not easy. But according to the *English*, a reflective Telescope of but five Feet, has the same Effect as another of an hundred Feet in Length.

LETTER XVII.

ON

INFINITES in GEOMETRY,

AND

Sir *Isaac Newton's*

CHRONOLOGY.

THE Labyrinth and Abyss of Infinity, is also a new Course Sir *Isaac Newton* has gone through, and we are oblig'd to him for the Clue by whose Assistance we are enabled to trace its various Windings.

DES CARTES got the Start of him also in this astonishing Invention. He advanc'd with mighty Steps in his Geometry, and was arriv'd at the very Borders of Infinity, but went no farther. Dr. *Wallis* about the Middle of the last Century, was the first who reduc'd a Fraction by a perpetual Division to an infinite Series.

T H E Lord *Brounker* employ'd this Series to square the Hyperbola.

M E R C A T O R publish'd a Demonstration of this Quadrature, much about which Time, Sir *Isaac Newton* being then twenty three Years of Age, had invented a general Method to perform, on all geometrical Curves, what had just before been try'd on the Hyperbola.

'T I S to this Method of subjecting every where Infinity to algebraical Calculations, that the Name is given of differential Calculations or of Fluxions, and integral Calculation. 'Tis the Art of numbring and measuring exactly a Thing whose Existence cannot be conceiv'd.

A N D, indeed, would you not imagine that a Man laugh'd at you, who should declare that there are Lines infinitely great which form an Angle infinitely little?

T H A T a right Line, which is a right Line so long as it is finite, by changing infinitely little its Direction, becomes an infinite Curve; and that a Curve may become infinitely less than another Curve?

T H A T there are infinite Squares, infinite Cubes; and Infinites of Infinites all greater than one another, and the last but one of which, is nothing in Comparison of the last?

A L L these Things which at first appear to be the utmost Excess of Frenzy, are in reality an Effort of the Subtilty and Extent of the human Mind, and the Art of finding Truths which till then had been unknown.

THIS so bold Edifice is even founded on simple Ideas. The Business is to measure the Diagonal of a Square, to give the Area of a Curve, to find the square Root of a Number, which has none in common Arithmetic. After all, the Imagination ought not to be startled any more at so many Orders of Infinites, than at the so well known Proposition, *viz.* that Curve Lines may always be made to pass between a Circle and a Tangent; or at that other, namely that Matter is divisible in *infinitum.* These two Truths have been demonstrated many Years, and are no less incomprehensible than the Things we have been speaking of.

FOR many Years the Invention of this famous Calculation was denied Sir *Isaac Newton.* In *Germany* Mr. *Leibnitz* was consider'd as the Inventor of the Differences or Moments, call'd *Fluxions, and Mr. *Bernouilli* claim'd the integral Calculation. However, Sir *Isaac* is now thought to have first made the Discovery, and the other two have the Glory of having once made the World doubt whether 'twas to be ascrib'd to him or them. Thus some contested with Dr. *Harvey* the Invention of the Circulation of the Blood, as others disputed with Mr. *Perrault* that of the Circulation of the Sap.

HARTSOCHER and *Lewenhoeck* disputed with each other the Honour of having first seen the *Vermiculi* of which Mankind are form'd.

---

* By Sir *Isaac Newton.*

This *Hartsocher* also contested with *Huygens* the Invention of a new Method of calculating the Distance of a fix'd Star. 'Tis not yet known to what Philosopher we owe the Invention of the Cycloid.

BE this as it will, 'tis by the Help of this Geometry of Infinites that Sir *Isaac Newton* attain'd to the most sublime Discoveries. I am now to speak of another Work, which tho' more adapted to the Capacity of the human Mind, does nevertheless display some Marks of that creative Genius with which Sir *Isaac Newton* was inform'd in all his Researches. The Work I mean is a Chronology of a new kind, for what Province soever he undertook, he was sure to change the Ideas and Opinions receiv'd by the rest of Men.

ACCUSTOM'D to unravel and disintangle Chaos's, he was resolv'd to convey at least some Light into that of the Fables of Antiquity which are blended and confounded with History, and fix an uncertain Chronology. 'Tis true, that there is no Family, City or Nation, but endeavours to remove its Original as far backward as possible. Besides, the first Historians were the most negligent in setting down the Æra's; Books were infinitely less common than they are at this Time, and consequently Authors being not so obnoxious to Censure, they therefore impos'd upon the World with greater Impunity; and as 'tis evident that these have related a great

Number of fictitious Particulars, 'tis probable enough that they also gave us several false Æra's.

I T appear'd in general to Sir *Isaac*, that the World was five hundred Years younger than Chronologers declare it to be. He grounds his Opinion on the ordinary Course of Nature, and on the Observations which Astronomers have made.

B Y the Course of Nature we here understand the Time that every Generation of Men lives upon the Earth. The *Egyptians* first employ'd this vague and uncertain Method of calculating, when they began to write the Beginning of their History. These computed three hundred and forty one Generations from *Menes* to *Sethon*; and having no fix'd Æra, they suppos'd three Generations to consist of an hundred Years. In this Manner they computed eleven thousand three hundred and forty Years from *Menes's* Reign to that of *Sethon*.

T H E *Greeks* before they counted by Olympiads, follow'd the Method of the *Egyptians*, and even gave a little more Extent to Generations, making each to consist of forty Years.

N o w here both the *Egyptians* and the *Greeks* made an erroneous Computation. 'Tis true indeed, that according to the usual Course of Nature three Generations last about an hundred and twenty Years: But three Reigns are far from taking up so many. 'Tis very evident, that Mankind in general live longer than Kings are found to reign: So that an Author who should write a History, in which there were no Dates fix'd, and should know that nine Kings had reign'd over a Nation; such an Historian, would commit a great Error should he allow three hundred Years to these nine Monarchs. Every Generation takes about thirty six Years; every Reign is, one with the other, about twenty. Thirty Kings of *England* have sway'd the Scepter from *William* the Conqueror to *George* the First, the Years of whose Reigns added together, amount to six hundred and forty eight Years; which being divided equally among the thirty Kings, give to every one a Reign of twenty one Years and a half very near. Sixty three Kings of *France* have sat upon the Throne; these have, one with another, reign'd about twenty Years each. This is the usual Course of Nature: The Ancients therefore were mistaken, when they suppos'd the Durations in general, of Reigns, to equal that of Generations. They therefore allow'd too great a Number of Years, and consequently some Years must be substracted from their Computation.

ASTRONOMICAL Observations seem to have lent a still greater Assistance to our Philosopher. He appears to us stronger when he fights upon his own Ground.

YOU know that the Earth, besides its annual Motion which carries it round the Sun from West to East in the Space of a Year, has also a singular Revolution which was quite unknown till within these late Years. Its Poles have a very slow retrograde Motion from East to West, whence it happens that their Position every Day does not correspond exactly with the same Point of the Heavens. This Difference which is so insensible in a Year, becomes pretty considerable in Time; and in threescore and twelve Years the Difference is found to be of one Degree, that is to say, the three hundred and sixtieth Part of the Circumference of the whole Heaven. Thus after seventy two Years the *Colure* of the vernal Equinox which pass'd thro' a fix'd Star, corresponds with another fix'd Star. Hence it is, that the Sun, instead of being in that Part of the Heavens in which the *Ram* was situated in the Time of *Hipparchus*, is found to correspond with that Part of the Heavens in which the *Bull* was situated; and the *Twins* are plac'd where the *Bull* then stood. All the Signs have chang'd their Situation, and yet we still retain the same Manner of speaking as the Ancients did. In this Age we say that the Sun is in the *Ram* in the Spring, from the same Principle of Condescension that we say that the Sun turns round.

HIPPARCHUS was the first among the *Greeks* who observ'd some Change in the Constellations with regard to the Equinoxes, or rather who learnt it from the *Egyptians*. Philosophers ascrib'd this Motion to the Stars; for

in those Ages People were far from imagining
such a Revolution in the Earth, which was suppos'd to be immoveable in every respect. They
therefore created a Heaven in which they fix'd
the several Stars, and gave this Heaven a particular Motion by which it was carried towards
the East, whilst that all the Stars seem'd to perform their diurnal Revolution from East to
West. To this Error they added a second of
much greater Consequence, by imagining that
the pretended Heaven of the fix'd Stars advanc'd
one Degree eastward every hundred Years. In
this Manner they were no less mistaken in their
astronomical Calculation than in their System
of Natural Philosophy. As for Instance, an
Astronomer in that Age would have said, that
the Vernal Equinox was in the Time of such
and such an Observation, in such a Sign, and
in such a Star. It has advanc'd two Degrees of
each since the Time that Observation was made to
the present. Now two Degrees are equivalent to
two hundred Years; consequently the Astronomer
who made that Observation liv'd just so many
Years before me. 'Tis certain that an Astronomer
who had argued in this Manner would have
mistook just fifty four Years; hence it is that the
Ancients, who were doubly deceiv'd, made their
great Year of the World, that is, the Revolution
of the whole Heavens, to consist of thirty six
thousand Years. But the Moderns are sensible
that this imaginary Revolution of the Heaven

of the Stars, is nothing else than the Revolution of the Poles of the Earth, which is perform'd in twenty five thousand nine hundred Years. It may be proper to observe transiently in this Place, that Sir *Isaac*, by determining the Figure of the Earth, has very happily explain'd the Cause of this Revolution.

A L L this being laid down, the only Thing remaining to settle Chronology, is, to see thro' what Star, the *Colure* of the Equinoxes passes, and where it intersects at this Time the Ecliptick in the Spring; and to discover whether some ancient Writer does not tell us in what Point the Ecliptic was intersected in his Time, by the same *Colure* of the Equinoxes.

C L E M E N S   A L E X A N D R I N U S informs us, that *Chiron*, who went with the *Argonauts*, observ'd the Constellations at the Time of that famous Expedition, and fix'd the vernal Equinox to the Middle of the *Ram*; the autumnal Equinox to the Middle of *Libra*; our Summer Solstice to the Middle of *Cancer*, and our Winter Solstice to the Middle of *Capricorn*.

A L O N G Time after the Expedition of the *Argonauts*, and a Year before the *Peloponnesian* War, *Methon* observ'd that the Point of the Summer Solstice pass'd thro' the eighth Degree of *Cancer*.

Now every Sign of the Zodiack contains thirty Degrees. In *Chiron's* Time, the Solstice was arriv'd at the Middle of the Sign, that is to say to the fifteenth Degree. A Year before the *Peloponnesian* War it was at the eighth, and therefore it had retarded seven Degrees. A Degree is equivalent to seventy two Years; consequently, from the Beginning of the *Peloponnesian* War to the Expedition of the *Argonauts*, there is no more than an Interval of seven times seventy two Years, which make five hundred and four Years, and not seven hundred Years, as the *Greeks* computed. Thus in comparing the Position of the Heavens at this Time, with their Position in that Age, we find that the Expedition of the *Argonauts* ought to be plac'd about nine hundred Years before *Christ*, and not about fourteen hundred; and consequently that the World is not so old by five hundred Years as it was generally suppos'd to be. By this Calculation all the Æra's are drawn nearer, and the several Events are found to have happen'd later than is computed. I don't know whether this ingenious System will be favourably receiv'd; and whether these Notions will prevail so far with the Learned, as to prompt them to reform the Chronology of the World. Perhaps these Gentlemen would think it too great a Condescension, to allow one and the same Man the Glory of having improv'd natural Philosophy, Geometry and History. This would be a kind of universal Monarchy, which the Principle of Self-Love that is in Man, will scarce suffer him to indulge his Fellow-Creature; and, indeed, at the same Time that some very great Philosophers attack'd Sir *Isaac Newton's* attractive Principle, others fell upon his chronological System. Time that shou'd discover to which of these the Victory is due, may perhaps only leave the Dispute still more undetermin'd.

LETTER XVIII.

ON

TRAGEDY.

THE *English* as well as the *Spaniards* were possess'd of Theatres, at a Time when the French had no more than moving, itinerant Stages. *Shakespear*, who was consider'd as the *Corneille* of the first mention'd Nation, was pretty near Cotemporary with *Lopez de Vega*, and he created, as it were, the *English* Theatre. *Shakespear* boasted a strong, fruitful Genius: He was natural and sublime, but had not so much as a single Spark of good Taste, or knew one Rule of the Drama. I will now hazard a random, but, at the same Time, true Reflection, which is, that the great Merit of this Dramatic Poet has been the Ruin of the *English* Stage. There are such beautiful, such noble, such dreadful Scenes in this Writer's monstrous Farces, to which the Name of Tragedy is given, that they have always been exhibited with great Success. Time, which only gives Reputation to

Writers, at last makes their very Faults venerable. Most of the whimsical, gigantic Images of
this Poet, have, thro' Length of Time (it being
an hundred and fifty Years since they were first
drawn) acquir'd a Right of passing for sublime.
Most of the modern dramatic Writers have
copied him; but the Touches and Descriptions
which are applauded in *Shakespear*, are hiss'd
at in these Writers; and you'll easily believe
that the Veneration in which this Author is held,
increases in Proportion to the Contempt which
is shown to the Moderns. Dramatic Writers
don't consider that they should not imitate
him; and the ill Success of *Shakespear's* Imita-
tors, produces no other Effect, than to make
him be consider'd as inimitable. You remember
that in the Tragedy of OTHELLO *Moor of* Venice,
(a most tender Piece) a Man strangles his Wife
on the Stage; and that the poor Woman, whilst
she is strangling, cries aloud, that she dies very
unjustly. You know that in HAMLET *Prince of*
Denmark, two Grave-Diggers made a Grave,
and are all the Time drinking, singing Ballads,
and making humourous Reflexions, (natural
indeed enough to Persons of their Profession)
on the several Skulls they throw up with their
Spades; but a Circumstance which will surprize
you is, that this ridiculous Incident has been
imitated. In the Reign of King *Charles* the
Second, which was that of Politeness, and the
Golden Age of the Liberal Arts; *Otway*, in his

VENICE PRESERV'D, introduces *Antonio* the Senator, and *Naki* his Curtezan, in the Midst of the Horrors of the Marquis of *Bedemar's* Conspiracy. *Antonio*, the superannuated Senator plays, in his Mistress's Presence, all the apish Tricks of a lewd, impotent Debauchee who is quite frantic and out of his Senses. He mimicks a Bull and a Dog; and bites his Mistress's Leg, who kicks and whips him. However, the Players have struck these Buffooneries (which indeed were calculated merely for the Dregs of the People) out of *Otway's* Tragedy; but they have still left in *Shakespear's* JULIUS CÆSAR, the Jokes of the *Roman* Shoemakers and Coblers, who are introduc'd in the same Scene with *Brutus* and *Cassius*. You will undoubtedly complain that those who have hitherto discours'd with you on the *English* Stage, and especially on the celebrated *Shakespear*, have taken Notice only of his Errors; and that no one has translated any of those strong, those forcible Passages which atone for all his Faults. But to this I will answer, that nothing is easier than to exhibit in Prose all the silly Impertinencies which a Poet may have thrown out; but that 'tis a very difficult Task to translate his fine Verses. All your junior academical *Sophs*, who set up for Censors of the eminent Writers, compile whole Volumes; but methinks two Pages which display some of the Beauties of great Genius's, are of infinitely more Value than all the idle Rhapsodies of those

Commentators; and I will join in Opinion with all Persons of good Taste in declaring, that greater Advantage may be reap'd from a Dozen Verses of *Homer* or *Virgil*, than from all the Critiques put together which have been made on those two great Poets.

I HAVE ventur'd to translate some Passages of the most celebrated *English* Poets, and shall now give you one from *Shakespear*. Pardon the Blemishes of the Translation for the Sake of the Original; and remember always that when you see a Version, you see merely a faint Print of a beautiful Picture. I have made Choice of Part of the celebrated Soliloquy in *Hamlet*, which you may remember is as follows.

> *To be, or not to be! that is the Question!*
> *Whether 'tis nobler in the Mind to suffer*
> *The Stings and Arrows of outrageous Fortune,*
> *Or to take Arms against a Sea of Troubles,*
> *And by opposing, end them? To dye! to sleep!*
> *No more! and by a Sleep to say we end*
> *The Heart-ach, and the thousand natural*
> *   Shocks*
> *That Flesh is Heir to! 'Tis a Consummation*
> *Devoutly to be wish'd. To die! to sleep!*
> *To sleep, perchance to dream! Ay, there's the*
> *   Rub;*
> *For in that Sleep of Death, what Dreams may*
> *   come*
> *When we have shuffled off this mortal Coyle,*

Must give us Pause. There's the respect
That makes Calamity of so long Life:
For who wou'd bear the Whips and Scorns of
 Time,
Th' Oppressor's Wrong, the poor Man's con-
 tumely,
The Pangs of despis'd Love, the Laws Delay,
The Insolence of Office, and the Spurns
That patient Merit of th' unworthy takes,
When by himself might his Quietus make
With a bare Bodkin? Who would these Fardles
 bear
To groan and sweat under a weary Life,
But that the Dread of something after Death,
The undiscover'd Country, from whose Bourn
No traveller returns, puzzles the Will,
And makes us rather bear those Ills we have,
Than fly to others that we know not of?
Thus Conscience does make Cowards of us all;
And thus the native Hue of Resolution
Is sicklied o'er with the pale Cast of Thought;
And Enterprizes of great Weight and Moment
With this Regard their Currents turn away,
And lose the Name of Action——

My Version of it runs thus:

Demeure, il faut choisir & passer à l'instant
De la vie, à la mort, ou de l'Etre au neant.
Dieux cruels, s'il en est, éclairez mon courage.
Faut-il vieillir courbé sous la main qui m'out-
 rage,

Supporter, ou finir mon malheur & mon sort?
Qui suis je? Qui m'arrete! & qu'est ce que la
      Mort?
C'est la fin de nos maux, c'est mon unique
      Azile
Après de long transports, c'est un sommeil
      tranquile.
On s'endort, & tout meurt, mais un affreux
      reveil
Doit succeder peut etre aux douceurs du
      sommeil!
On nous menace, on dit que cette courte Vie,
De tourmens éternels est aussi-tôt-suivie.
O Mort! moment fatal! affreuse Eternité!
Tout cœur à ton seul nom se glace épouvanté.
Eh! qui pourroit sans Toi supporter cette vie,
De nos Prêtres menteurs benir l'hypocrisie;
D'une indigne Maitresse encenser les erreurs,
Ramper sous un Ministre, adorer ses hauteurs;
Et montrer les langueurs de son ame abattue,
A des Amis ingrats qui detournent la vue?
La Mort seroit trop douce en ces extrémitez,
Mais le scrupule parle, & nous crie, Arrêtez;
Il defend à nos mains cet heureux homicide
Et d'un Heros guerrier, fait un Chrétien
      timide, &c.

DON'T imagine that I have translated *Shakespear* in a servile Manner. Woe to the Writer who gives a literal Verison; who by rendring every Word of his Original, by that very means enervates the Sense, and extinguishes all the Fire of it. 'Tis on such an Occasion one may justly affirm, that the Letter kills, but the Spirit quickens.

HERE follows another Passage copied from a celebrated Tragic Writer among the *English*. 'Tis *Dryden*, a Poet in the Reign of *Charles* the Second; a Writer whose Genius was too exuberant, and not accompanied with Judgment enough. Had he writ only a tenth Part of the Works he left behind him, his Character wou'd have been conspicuous in every Part; but his great Fault is his having endeavour'd to be universal.

THE Passage in Question is as follows:

When I consider Life, 'tis all a Cheat,
Yet fool'd by Hope, Men favour the Deceit;
Trust on and think, to Morrow will repay;
To Morrow's falser than the former Day;
Lies more; and whilst it says we shall be blest
With some new Joy, cuts off what we possest;
Strange Cozenage! none wou'd live past Years
    again,
Yet all hope Pleasure in what yet remain,
And from the Dregs of Life think to receive
What the first sprightly Running could not
    give.
I'm tir'd with waiting for this chymic Gold,
Which fools us young, and beggars us when old.

I shall now give you my Translation:

De desseins en regrets & d'erreurs en desirs
Les Mortels insenses promenent leur Folie.
Dans des malheurs presents, dans l'espoir des
    plaisirs
Nous ne vivons jamais, nous attendons la vie.
Demain, demain, dit-on, va combler tous nos
    vœux.
Demain vient, & nous laisse encore plus mal-
    heureux.
Quelle est l'erreur, helas! du soin qui nous
    dévore.
Nul de nous ne voudroit recommencer son cours,
De nos premiers momens nous maudissons
    l'aurore,
Et de la nuit qui vient, nous attendons encore
Ce qu'ont en vain promis les plus beaux de nos
    jours, &c.

'TIS in these detach'd Passages that the
English have hitherto excell'd. Their dramatic
Pieces, most of which are barbarous and without Decorum, Order or Verisimilitude, dart
such resplendent Flashes, thro' this Gloom, as
amaze and astonish. The Style is too much in-
flated, too unnatural, too closely copied from
the *Hebrew* Writers, who abound so much with
the *Asiatic* Fustian. But then it must be also
confess'd, that the *Stilts* of the figurative Style
on which the *English* Tongue is lifted up, raises
the Genius at the same Time very far aloft, tho'
with an irregular Pace. The first *English* Writer

who compos'd a regular Tragedy and infus'd a Spirit of Elegance thro' every Part of it, was the illustrious Mr. *Addison*. His CATO is a Master-piece both with regard to the Diction, and to the Beauty and Harmony of the Numbers. The Character of *Cato* is, in my Opinion, vastly superior to that of *Cornelia* in the POMPEY of *Corneille :* For *Cato* is great without any Thing like Fustian, and *Cornelia*, who besides is not a necessary Character, tends sometimes to bombast. Mr. *Addison's Cato* appears to me the greatest Character that was ever brought upon any Stage, but then the rest of them don't correspond to the Dignity of it : And this dramatic Piece so excellently well writ, is disfigur'd by a dull Love-Plot, which spreads a certain Languor over the whole, that quite murders it.

T H E Custom of introducing Love at random and at any rate in the Drama, pass'd from *Paris* to *London* about 1660, with our Ribbons and our Peruques. The Ladies who adorn the Theatrical Circle, there, in like Manner as in this City, will suffer Love only to be the Theme of every Conversation. The judicious Mr. *Addison* had the effeminate Complaisance to soften the Severity of his dramatic Character so, as to adapt it to the Manners of the Age; and from an Endeavour to please, quite ruin'd a Master-Piece in its kind. Since his Time, the Drama is become more regular, the Audience more difficult to be pleas'd, and Writers more

correct and less bold. I have seen some new
Pieces that were written with great Regularity,
but which at the same Time were very flat and
insipid. One would think that the *English* had
been hitherto form'd to produce irregular Beauties only. The shining Monsters of *Shakespear*,
give infinite more Delight than the judicious
Images of the Moderns. Hitherto the poetical
Genius of the *English* resembles a tufted Tree
planted by the Hand of Nature, that throws out
a thousand Branches at random, and spreads
unequally, but with great Vigour. It dies if you
attempt to force its Nature, and to lop and dress
it in the same Manner as the Trees of the Garden
of *Marli*.

L E T T E R X I X.

O N

C O M E D Y.

I A M surpriz'd that the judicious and in-genious Mr. *de Muralt*, who has publish'd some Letters on the *English* and *French* Nations, should have confin'd himself, in treat-ing of Comedy, merely to censure *Shadwell* the comic Writer. This Author was had in pretty Contempt in Mr. *de Muralt's* Time, and was not the Poet of the polite Part of the Nation. His dramatic Pieces which pleas'd some Time in acting, were despis'd by all Persons of Taste and might be compar'd to many Plays which I have seen in *France*, that drew Crowds to the Play-house, at the same Time that they were intolerable to read; and of which it might be said, that the whole City of *Paris* exploded them, and yet all flock'd to see 'em represented on the Stage. Methinks Mr. *de Muralt* should have mention'd an excellent comic Writer (living when he was in *England*) I mean Mr. *Wycherley*, who was a long Time known publickly to be happy in the good Graces of the most celebrated Mistress of King *Charles* the Second. This Gentleman who pass'd his Life among Persons of the highest Distinction, was perfectly well acquainted with their Lives and their Follies, and painted them with the strongest Pencil, and in the truest Colours. He has drawn a *Misantrope* or Man-hater, in Imitation of that of *Moliere*. All *Wycherley's* Strokes are stronger and bolder than those of our *Misantrope*, but then they are less delicate, and the Rules of Decorum are not so well observ'd in this Play. The *English* Writer has corrected the only Defect that is in *Moliere's* Comedy, the Thinness of the Plot, which also is so dispos'd that the Characters in it do not enough raise our Concern. The *English* Comedy affects us, and the Contrivance of the Plot is very ingenious, but at the same Time 'tis too bold for the *French* Manners. The Fable is this.—— A Captain of a Man of War, who is very brave, open-hearted, and enflam'd with a Spirit of Contempt for all Mankind, has a prudent, sincere Friend whom he yet is suspicious of, and a Mistress that loves him with the utmost Excess of Passion. The Captain so far from returning her Love, will not even condescend to look upon her; but confides intirely in a false Friend, who is the most worthless Wretch living. At the same Time he has given his Heart to a Creature who is the greatest Coquet, and the most perfidious of her Sex, and is so credulous as to be confident she is a *Penelope*, and his false Friend a *Cato*. He embarks on board his Ship in order to go and fight the *Dutch*, having left all his Money, his Jewels and every Thing he had in the World to this virtuous Creature, whom at the same Time he recommends to the Care of his suppos'd faithful Friend. Nevertheless the real Man of Honour whom he suspects so unaccountably, goes on board the Ship with him; and the Mistress on whom he would not bestow so much as one Glance, disguises herself in the Habit of a Page, and is with him the whole Voyage, without his once knowing that she is of a Sex different from that she attempts to pass for, which, by the Way, is not over natural.

THE Captain having blown up his own Ship in an Engagement, returns to *England* abandon'd and undone, accompanied by his Page and his Friend, without knowing the Friendship of the one, or the tender Passion of the other. Immediately he goes to the Jewel among Women, who he expected had preserv'd her Fidelity to him, and the Treasure he had left in her Hands. He meets with her indeed, but married to the honest Knave in whom he had repos'd so much Confidence; and finds she had acted as treacherously with regard to the Casket he had entrusted her with. The Captain can scarce think it possible, that a Woman of Virtue and Honour can

act so vile a Part; but to convince him still more
of the Reality of it, this very worthy Lady falls
in Love with the little Page, and will force him
to her Embraces. But as it is requisite Justice
should be done, and that in a dramatick Piece
Virtue ought to be rewarded and Vice punish'd; 'tis at last found that the Captain takes
his Page's Place, and lyes with his faithless
Mistress, cuckolds his treacherous Friend,
thrusts his Sword through his Body, recovers
his Casket and marries his Page. You'll observe
that this Play is also larded with a petulant,
litigious old Woman (a Relation of the Captain)
who is the most comical Character that was ever
brought upon the Stage.

W Y C H E R L E Y has also copied from *Moliere* another Play, of as singular and bold a Cast,
which is a kind of *Ecole des Femmes*, or, *School
for married Women*.

T H E principal Character in this Comedy is
one *Horner*, a sly Fortune-Hunter, and the
Terror of all the City Husbands. This Fellow
in order to play a surer Game, causes a Report
to be spread, that in his last Illness, the Surgeons
had found it necessary to have him made an
Eunuch. Upon his appearing in this noble Character, all the Husbands in Town flock to him
with their Wives, and now poor *Horner* is only
puzzled about his Choice. However, he gives
the Preference particularly to a little female
Peasant; a very harmless, innocent Creature,

who enjoys a fine Flush of Health, and cuckolds her Husband with a Simplicity that has infinitely more Merit than the witty Malice of the most experienc'd Ladies. This Play cannot indeed be call'd the School of good Morals, but 'tis certainly the School of Wit and true Humour.

S I R *John Vanbrugh* has writ several Comedies which are more humourous than those of Mr. *Wycherley*, but not so ingenious. Sir *John* was a Man of Pleasure, and likewise a Poet and an Architect. The general Opinion is, that he is as sprightly in his Writings as he is heavy in his Buildings. 'Tis he who rais'd the famous Castle of *Blenheim*, a ponderous and lasting Monument of our unfortunate Battle of *Hockstet*. Were the Apartments but as spacious as the Walls are thick, this Castle wou'd be commodious enough. Some Wag, in an Epitaph he made on Sir *John Vanbrugh*, has these Lines:

> *Earth lye light on him, for he*
> *Laid many a heavy Load on thee.*

S I R *John* having taken a Tour into *France* before the glorious War that broke out in 1701, was thrown into the *Bastile*, and detain'd there for some Time, without being ever able to discover the Motive which had prompted our Ministry to indulge him this Mark of their Distinction. He writ a Comedy during his Confinement; and a Circumstance which appears to me very extraordinary is, that we don't meet

with so much as a single satyrical Stroke against
the Country in which he had been so injuriously
treated.

THE late Mr. *Congreve* rais'd the Glory of
Comedy to a greater Height than any English
Writer before or since his Time. He wrote only
a few Plays, but they are all excellent in their
kind. The Laws of the Drama are strictly observ'd in them; they abound with Characters all
which are shadow'd with the utmost Delicacy,
and we don't meet with so much as one low,
or coarse Jest. The Language is every where
that of Men of Honour, but their Actions are
those of Knaves; a Proof that he was perfectly
well acquainted with human Nature, and frequented what we call polite Company. He was
infirm, and come to the Verge of Life when I
knew him. Mr. *Congreve* had one Defect, which
was, his entertaining too mean an Idea of his
first Profession, (that of a Writer) tho' 'twas to
this he ow'd his Fame and Fortune. He spoke
of his Works as of Trifles that were beneath
him; and hinted to me in our first Conversation,
that I should visit him upon no other Foot than
that of a Gentleman, who led a Life of Plainness and Simplicity. I answer'd, that had he
been so unfortunate as to be a mere Gentleman
I should never have come to see him; and I was
very much disgusted at so unseasonable a Piece
of Vanity.

MR. *Congreve's* Comedies are the most witty

and regular, those of Sir *John Vanbrugh* most gay and humourous, and those of Mr. *Wycherley* have the greatest Force and Spirit. It may be proper to observe, that these fine Genius's never spoke disadvantageously of *Moliere*; and that none but the contemptible Writers among the *English* have endeavour'd to lessen the Character of that great comic Poet. Such *Italian* Musicians as despise *Lully* are themselves Persons of no Character or Ability; but a *Buononcini* esteems that great Artist, and does Justice to his Merit.

T H E *English* have some other good comic Writers living, such as Sir *Richard Steele*, and Mr. *Cibber*, who is an excellent Player, and also Poet Laureat, a Title which how ridiculous soever it may be thought, is yet worth a thousand Crowns a Year, (besides some considerable Privileges) to the Person who enjoys it. Our illustrious *Corneille* had not so much.

To conclude. Don't desire me to descend to Particulars with regard to these *English* Comedies, which I am so fond of applauding; nor to give you a single smart Saying, or humorous Stroke from *Wycherley* or *Congreve*. We don't laugh in reading a Translation. If you have a Mind to understand the *English* Comedy, the only way to do this will be for you to go to *England*, to spend three Years in *London*, to make your self Master of the *English* Tongue, and to frequent the Play-house every Night. I receive but little Pleasure from the Perusal of

Aristophanes and *Plautus*, and for this Reason, because I am neither a *Greek* nor a *Roman*. The Delicacy of the Humour, the Allusion, the *à propos*, all these are lost to a Foreigner.

BUT 'tis different with respect to Tragedy, this treating only of exalted Passions and heroical Follies, which the antiquated Errors of Fable or History have made sacred. *Oedipus*, *Electra* and such like Characters, may with as much Propriety, be treated of by the *Spaniards*, the *English*, or Us, as by the *Greeks*. But true Comedy is the speaking Picture of the Follies and ridiculous Foibles of a Nation; so that he only is able to judge of the Painting, who is perfectly acquainted with the People it represents.

LETTER XX.

On such of the

NOBILITY

As cultivate the

BELLES LETTRES.

THERE once was a Time in *France* when the polite Arts were cultivated by Persons of the highest Rank in the State. The Courtiers particularly, were conversant in them, altho' Indolence, a Taste for Trifles, and a Passion for Intrigue, were the Divinities of the Country. The Court methinks at this Time seems to have given into a Taste quite opposite to that of polite Literature, but perhaps the Mode of Thinking may be reviv'd in a little Time. The *French* are of so flexible a Disposition, may be moulded into such a Variety of Shapes, that the Monarch needs but command

and he is immediately obey'd. The *English* generally think, and Learning is had in greater Honour among them than in our Country; an Advantage that results naturally from the Form of their Government. There are about eight hundred Persons in *England* who have a Right to speak in publick, and to support the Interest of the Kingdom; and near five or six Thousand may in their Turns, aspire to the same Honour. The whole Nation set themselves up as Judges over these, and every Man has the Liberty of publishing his Thoughts with regard to publick Affairs; which shews, that all the People in general are indispensably oblig'd to cultivate their Understandings. In *England* the Governments of *Greece* and *Rome* are the Subject of every Conversation, so that every Man is under a Necessity of perusing such Authors as treat of them, how disagreeable soever it may be to him; and this Study leads naturally to that of polite Literature. Mankind in general speak well in their respective Professions. What is the Reason why our Magistrates, our Lawyers, our Physicians, and a great Number of the Clergy are abler Scholars, have a finer Taste and more Wit than Persons of all other Professions? The Reason is, because their Condition of Life requires a cultivated and enlightned Mind, in the same Manner as a Merchant is oblig'd to be acquainted with his Traffick. Not long since an *English* Nobleman, who was very young, came to see me at *Paris* in his Return from *Italy*. He had writ a poetical Description of that Country, which, for Delicacy and Politeness may vie with any Thing we meet with in the Earl of *Rochester.* or in our *Chaulieu,* our *Sarrasin,* or *Chapelle,* The Translation I have given of it is so inexpressive of the Strength and delicate Humour of the Original, that I am oblig'd seriously to ask Pardon of the Author, and of all who understand *English.* However, as this is the only Method I have to make his Lordship's Verses known, I shall here present you with them in our Tongue.

Qu'ay je donc vû dans l'Italie?
Orgueil, Astuce, & Pauvreté,
Grands Complimens, peu de Bonté
Et beaucoup de Ceremonie.

L'extravagante Comedie,
Que souvent l'Inquisition*
Veut qu'on nomme Religion;
Mais qu'ici nous nommons Folie.

La Nature en vain bienfaisante
Veut enricher ses Lieux charmans,
Des Prêtres la main desolante
Etouffe ses plus beaux présens.

* His Lordship undoubtedly hints at the Farces which certain Preachers act in the open Squares.

Les Monsignors, soy disant Grands,
Seuls dans leurs Palais magnifiques
Y sont d'illustres faineants,
Sans argent, & sans domestiques.

Pour les Petits, sans liberté,
Martyrs du joug qui les domine,
Ils ont fait vœu de pauvreté,
Priant Dieu par oisiveté
Et toûjours jeunant par famine.

Ces beaux lieux du Pape benis
Semblent habitez par les Diables ;
Et les Habitans miserables
Sont damnez dans le Paradis.

LETTER XXI.

ON THE

Earl of ROCHESTER

AND

Mr. *WALLER*.

THE Earl of *Rochester*'s Name is universally known. Mr. *de St. Evremont* has
made very frequent mention of him, but
then he has represented this famous Nobleman
in no other Light than as the Man of Pleasure,
as one who was the Idol of the Fair; but with
regard to my self, I would willingly describe in
him the Man of Genius, the great Poet. Among
other Pieces which display the shining Imagination his Lordship only cou'd boast, he wrote
some Satyrs on the same Subjects as those our
celebrated *Boileau* made choice of. I don't know
any better Method of improving the Taste, than to
compare the Productions of such great Genius's

as have exercis'd their Talent on the same Subject. *Boileau* declaims as follows against human
Reason in his Satyr on Man.

> *Cependant à le voir plein de vapeurs légeres,*
> *Soi-même se bercer de ses propres chimeres,*
> *Lui seul de la nature est la baze & l'appui,*
> *Et le dixieme ciel ne tourne que pour lui.*
> *De tous les Animaux il est ici le Maître;*
> *Qui pourroit le nier, poursuis tu? Moi peut-*
>   *être.*
> *Ce maître prétendu qui leur donne des loix,*
> *Ce Roi des Animaux, combien à-t'il de Rois?*

> *Yet, pleas's with idle Whimsies of his Brain,*
> *And puff'd with Pride, this haughty Thing*
>   *wou'd fain*
> *Be thought himself the only Stay and Prop*
> *That holds the mighty Frame of Nature up.*
> *The Skies and Stars his Properties must seem,*

> ———   ———   ———   —

> *Of all the Creatures he's the Lord, he cries.*

> ———   ———   ———

And who is there, *say you*, that dares deny
So own'd a Truth? That may be, Sir, do I.

———   ———   ———

> *This boasted Monarch of the World who awes*
> *The Creatures here, and with his Nod gives*
>   *Laws;*
> *This self-nam'd King, who thus pretends to be*
> *The Lord of all, how many Lords has he?*
>   OLDHAM a little alter'd.

THE Lord *Rochester* expresses himself, in his Satyr against Man, in pretty near the following Manner: But I must first desire you always to remember, that the Versions I give you from the *English* Poets are written with Freedom and Latitude; and that the Restraint of our Versification, and the Delicacies of the *French* Tongue, will not allow a Translator to convey into it the licentious Impetuosity and Fire of the *English* Numbers.

Cet Esprit que je hais, cet Esprit plein d'erreur,
Ce n'est pas ma raison, c'est la tienne Docteur.
C'est la raison frivôle, inquiete, orgeuilleuse
Des sages Animaux, rivale dédaigneuse,
Qui croit entr'eux & l'Ange, occuper le milieu,
Et pense être ici bas l'image de son Dieu.
Vil atôme imparfait, qui croit, doute, dispute
Rampe, s'eleve, tombe, & nie encore sa chûte.
Qui nous dit je suis libre, en nous montrant ses
        fers,
Et dont l'œil trouble & faux, croit percer
        l'univers.
Allez, reverends Fous, bienheureux Fanatiques,
Compilez bien l'Amas de vos Riens scholas-
        tiques,
Peres de Visions, & d'Enigmes sacrez,
Auteurs du Labirinthe, ou vous vous égarez.
Allez obscurement éclaircir vos misteres,
Et courez dans l'école adorer vos chimeres.
Il est d'autres erreurs, il est de ces dévots

Condamné par eux mêmes à l'ennui du repos.
Ce mystique encloîtré, fier de son Indolence
Tranquille, au sein de Dieu. Que peut il faire?
  Il pense.
Non, tu ne penses point, misérable, tu dors:
Inutile à la terre, & mis au rang des Morts.
Ton esprit énervé croupit dans la Molesse.
Reveille toi, sois homme, & sors de ton Yvresse.
L'homme est né pour agir, & tu pretens penser?
  &c.

The Original runs thus:

Hold, mighty Man, I cry all this we know,
And 'tis this very Reason I despise,
This supernatural Gift, that makes a Mite
Think he's the Image of the Infinite;
Comparing his short Life, void of all rest,
To the eternal and the ever blest.
This busy, puzzling Stirrer up of Doubt,
That frames deep Mysteries, then finds 'em out,
Filling, with frantic Crowds of thinking Fools,
Those reverend Bedlams, Colleges and Schools;
Borne on whose Wings, each heavy Sot can
    pierce
The Limits of the boundless Universe.
So charming Ointments make an old Witch fly,
And bear a crippled Carcass through the Sky.
'Tis this exalted Power, whose Business lies
In Nonsense and Impossibilities.
This made a whimsical Philosopher,

Before the spacious World his Tub prefer;
And we have modern cloyster'd Coxcombs, who
Retire to think, 'cause they have nought to do:
But Thoughts are giv'n for Action's Govern-
    ment,
Where Action ceases, Thought's impertinent.

WHETHER these Ideas are true or false, 'tis certain they are express'd with an Energy and Fire which form the Poet. I shall be very far from attempting to examine philosophically into these Verses; to lay down the Pencil and take up the Rule and Compass on this Occasion; my only Design in this Letter, being to display the Genius of the *English* Poets, and therefore I shall continue in the same View.

THE celebrated Mr. *Waller* has been very much talk'd of in *France*, and Mr. *de la Fontaine*, St. *Evremont* and *Bayle* have written his Elogium, but still his Name only is known. He had much the same Reputation in *London* as *Voiture* had in *Paris*, and in my Opinion deserv'd it better. *Voiture* was born in an Age that was just emerging from Barbarity; an Age that was still rude and ignorant, the People of which aim'd at Wit, tho' they had not the least Pretensions to it, and sought for Points and Conceits instead of Sentiments. *Bristol* Stones are more easily found than Diamonds. *Voiture*, born with an easy and frivolous Genius, was the first who shone in this Aurora of *French* Literature. Had he come into the World after those great Genius's who spread such a Glory over the Age of *Lewis* the Fourteenth, he would either have been un-known, wou'd have been despis'd, or wou'd have corrected his Style. *Boileau* applauded him, but 'twas in his first Satyrs, at a Time when the Taste of that great Poet was not yet form'd. He was young, and in an Age when Persons form a Judgment of Men from their Reputation, and not from their Writings. Besides, *Boileau* was very partial both in his Encomiums and his Censures. He applauded *Segrais*, whose Works no Body reads; he abus'd *Quinault*, whose poetical Pieces every one has got by Heart, and is wholly silent upon *La Fontaine*. *Waller*, tho' a better Poet than *Voiture*, was not yet a finish'd Poet. The Graces breathe in such of *Waller's* Works as are writ in a tender Strain, but then they are languid thro' Negligence, and often disfigur'd with false Thoughts. The *English* had not, in his Time, attain'd the Art of correct Writing. But his serious Compositions exhibit a Strength and Vigour which cou'd not have been expected from the Softness and Effeminacy of his other Pieces. He wrote an Elegy on *Oliver Cromwell*, which with all it's Faults is nevertheless look'd upon as a Master-Piece. To understand this Copy of Verses, you are to know that the Day *Oliver* died was remarkable for a great Storm. His Poem begins in this Manner:

Il n'est plus, s'en est fait, soumettons nous au
    sort,
Le ciel a signalé ce jour par des tempêtes,
Et la voix des tonnerres éclatant sur nos têtes
Vient d'annoncer sa mort.

Par ses derniers soupirs il ébranle cet île;
Cet île que son bras fit trembler tant de fois,
Quand dans le cours de ses Exploits,
Il brisoit la téte des Rois,
Et soumettoit un peuple à son joug seul docile.

Mer tu t'en és troublé; O Mer tes flots émus
Semblent dire en grondant aux plus lointains
    rivages
Que l'effroi de la terre & ton Maître n'est
    plus.

Tel au ciel autrefois s'envola Romulus,
Tel il quitta la Terre, au milieu des orages,
Tel d'un peuple guerrier il reçut les homages;
Obéï dans sa vie, à sa mort adoré,
Son palais fut un Temple, &c.

We must resign! Heav'n his great Soul does
    claim
In Storms as loud as his immortal Fame:
His dying Groans, his last Breath shakes our
    Isle,
And Trees uncut fall for his fun'ral Pile:
About his Palace their broad Roots are tost

Into the Air; so Romulus *was lost!*
New Rome *in such a Tempest miss'd her King,*
And from obeying fell to worshipping:
On Œta's *Top thus* Hercules *lay dead,*
With ruin'd Oaks and Pines about him spread.
Nature herself took Notice of his Death,
And, sighing, swell'd the Sea with such a
    Breath,
That to remotest Shores the Billows roul'd,
Th' approaching Fate of his great Ruler told.

WALLER.

'TWAS this Elogium that gave Occasion to
the Reply (taken Notice of in *Bayle*'s Dictionary)
which *Waller* made to King *Charles* the Second.
This King, to whom *Waller* had a little before,
(as is usual with Bards and Monarchs) presented
a Copy of Verses embroider'd with Praises;
reproach'd the Poet for not writing with so much
Energy and Fire as when he had applauded the
Usurper (meaning *Oliver;*) *Sir,* reply'd *Waller*
to the King, *we Poets succeed better in Fiction
than in Truth.* This Answer was not so sincere
as that which a *Dutch* Ambassador made, who,
when the same Monarch complain'd that his
Masters paid less Regard to him than they had
done to *Cromwell; Ah Sir!* says the Ambassador,
Oliver *was quite another Man* —— 'Tis not my
Intent to give a Commentary on *Waller*'s Character, nor on that of any other Person; for I
consider Men after their Death in no other Light

than as they were Writers, and wholly disregard every Thing else. I shall only observe, that *Waller*, tho' born in a Court, and to an Estate of five or six thousand Pounds Sterling a Year, was never so proud or so indolent as to lay aside the happy Talent which Nature had indulg'd him. The Earls of *Dorset* and *Roscommon*, the two Dukes of *Buckingham*, the Lord *Halifax* and so many other Noblemen, did not think the Reputation they obtain'd of very great Poets and illustrious Writers, any way derogatory to their Quality. They are more glorious for their Works than for their Titles. These cultivated the polite Arts with as much Assiduity, as tho' they had been their whole Dependance. They also have made Learning appear venerable in the Eyes of the Vulgar, who have need to be led in all Things by the Great; and who nevertheless fashion their Manners less after those of the Nobility (in *England* I mean) than in any other Country in the World.

LETTER XXII.

ON

Mr. *POPE*,

And some other FAMOUS

POETS.

INTENDED to treat of Mr. *Prior*, one of the most amiable *English* Poets, whom you saw Plenipotentiary and Envoy Extraordinary at *Paris* in 1712. I also design'd to have given you some Idea of the Lord *Roscommon*'s and the Lord *Dorset*'s Muse; but I find that to do this I should be oblig'd to write a large Volume, and that after much Pains and Trouble you wou'd have but an imperfect Idea of all those Works. Poetry is a kind of Music, in which a Man should have some Knowledge before he pretends to judge of it. When I gave you a Translation of some Passages from those foreign Poets, I only prick down, and that imperfectly, their Music; but then I cannot express the Taste of their Harmony.

THERE is one *English* Poem especially which I should despair of ever making you understand, the Title whereof is *Hudibras.* The Subject of it is the Civil War in the Time of the Grand Rebellion; and the Principles and Practice of the Puritans are therein ridicul'd. 'Tis *Don Quixot,* 'tis our * *Satyre Menippée* blended together. I never found so much Wit in one single Book as in that, which at the same Time is the most difficult to be translated. Who wou'd believe that a Work which paints in such lively and natural Colours the several Foibles and Follies of Mankind, and where we meet with more Sentiments than Words, should baffle the Endeavours of the ablest Translator? But the Reason of this is; almost every Part of it alludes to particular Incidents. The Clergy are there made the principal Object of Ridicule, which is understood but by few among the Laity. To explain this a Commentary would be requisite, and *Humour* when explain'd is no longer Hu-

---

* A Species of Satyr in Prose and Verse written in *France* in 1594, against the Chiefs of the League at that Time. This Satyr which is also call'd *Catholicon d'Espagne,* was look'd upon as a Master-piece. *Rapin, Le Roi, Pithou, Passerat* and *Chrétien,* the greatest Wits of that Age, are the Authors of it; and 'twas entitled *Ménippée,* from *Menippus,* a cynical Philosopher, who had written Letters fill'd with sharp, satyrical Expressions, in Imitation of *Varro,* who compos'd Satyrs which he entitled *Satyræ Menippeæ.*

mour. Whoever sets up for a Commentator of smart Sayings and Repartees, is himself a Blockhead. This is the Reason why the Works of the ingenious Dean *Swift*, who has been call'd the *English Rabelais*, will never be well understood in *France*. This Gentleman has the Honour (in common with *Rabelais*) of being a Priest, and like him laughs at every Thing. But in my humble Opinion, the Title of the *English Rabelais* which is given the Dean, is highly derogatory to his Genius. The former has interspers'd his unaccountably-fantastic and unintelligible Book, with the most gay Strokes of Humour, but which at the same Time has a greater Proportion of Impertinence. He has been vastly lavish of Erudition, of Smut, and insipid Raillery. An agreeable Tale of two Pages is purchas'd at the Expence of whole Volumes of Nonsense. There are but few Persons, and those of a grotesque Taste, who pretend to understand, and to esteem this Work; for as to the rest of the Nation, they laugh at the pleasant and diverting Touches which are found in *Rabelais* and despise his Book. He is look'd upon as the Prince of Buffoons. The Readers are vex'd to think that a Man who was Master of so much Wit should have made so wretched a Use of it. He is an intoxicated Philosopher, who never writ but when he was in Liquor.

D E A N *Swift* is *Rabelais* in his Senses, and frequenting the politest Company. The former indeed is not so gay as the latter, but then he possesses all the Delicacy, the Justness, the Choice, the good Taste, in all which Particulars our giggling rural Vicar *Rabelais* is wanting. The poetical Numbers of Dean *Swift* are of a singular and almost inimitable Taste; true Humour whether in Prose or Verse, seems to be his peculiar Talent, but whoever is desirous of understanding him perfectly, must visit the Island in which he was born.

'T WILL be much easier for you to form an Idea of Mr. *Pope*'s Works. He is in my Opinion the most elegant, the most correct Poet; and at the same Time the most harmonious (a Circumstance which redounds very much to the Honour of this Muse) that *England* ever gave Birth to. He has mellow'd the harsh Sounds of the *English* Trumpet to the soft Accents of the Flute. His Compositions may be easily translated, because they are vastly clear and perspicuous; besides, most of his Subjects are general, and relative to all Nations.

H I s *Essay on Criticism* will soon be known in *France*, by the Translation which *l'Abbé de Renel* has made of it.

H E R E is an Extract from his Poem entitled the *Rape of the Lock*, which I just now translated with the Latitude I usually take on these Occasions; for once again, nothing can be more ridiculous than to translate a Poet literally.

UMBRIEL, *à l'instant, vieil Gnome rechigné,*
Va d'une aîle pesante & d'un air renfrogné
Chercher en murmurant la Caverne profonde,
Où loin des doux raïons que répand l'œil du
*   monde*
La Déesse aux vapeurs a choisi son séjour.
Les tristes Aquilons y siflent à l'entour
Et le soufle mal sain de leur aride haleine
Y porte aux environs la fievre & la migraine.
Sur un riche Sofa derriere un Paravent
Loin des flambeaux, du bruit, des parleurs &
*   du vent,*
La quinteuse Déesse incessamment repose,
Le cœur gros de chagrin, sans en savoir la
*   cause.*
N'aiant pensé jamais, l'esprit toujours troublé,
L'œil chargé, le teint pâle, & l'hypocondre
*   enflé.*
La medisante Envie, est assise auprès d'elle,
Vieil spectre féminin, décrépite pucelle,
Avec un air devot déchirant son prochain,
Et chansonnant les Gens l'Evangile à la main.
Sur un lit plein de fleurs negligemment panchée
Une jeune Beauté non loin d'elle est couchée,
C'est l'Affectation qui grassaïe en parlant,
Ecoute sans entendre, & lorgne en regardant.
Qui rougit sans pudeur, & rit de tout sans joïe,
De cent maux différens prétend qu'elle est la
*   proïe;*
Et pleine de santé sous le rouge & le fard,
Se plaint avec molesse, & se pame avec Art.

U M B R I E L, *a dusky, melancholy Sprite*
As ever sullied the fair Face of Light,
Down to the central Earth, his proper Scene,
Repairs to search the gloomy Cave of Spleen.
Swift on his sooty Pinions flits the Gnome,
And in a Vapour reach'd the dismal Dome.
No chearful Breeze this sullen Region knows,
The dreaded East is all the Wind that blows.
Here, in a Grotto, shelter'd close from Air,
And screen'd in Shades from Day's detested
    Glare,
She sighs for ever on her pensive Bed,
Pain *at her Side, and* Megrim *at her Head,*
Two Handmaids wait the Throne. Alike in Place.
But diff'ring far in Figure and in Face,
Here stood Ill-nature *like an ancient Maid,*
Her wrinkled Form in black and white array'd;
With Store of Prayers for Mornings, Nights,
    and Noons,
Her Hand is fill'd; her Bosom with Lampoons.
There Affectation, *with a sickly Mien,*
Shows in her Cheek the Roses of eighteen,
Practis'd to lisp, and hang the Head aside,
Faints into Airs, and languishes with Pride;
On the Rich Quilt sinks with becoming Woe,
Wrapt in a Gown, for Sickness and for Show.

This Extract in the Original, (not in the faint
Translation I have given you of it) may be compar'd to the Description of *La Molesse* (Softness
or Effeminacy) in *Boileau's Lutrin.*

METHINKS I now have given you Specimens enough from the *English* Poets. I have made some transient mention of their Philosophers, but as for good Historians among them, I don't know of any; and indeed a *French* Man was forc'd to write their History. Possibly the *English* Genius, which is either languid or impetuous, has not yet requir'd that unaffected Eloquence, that plain but majestic Air which History requires. Possibly too, the Spirit of Party which exhibits Objects in a dim and confus'd Light, may have sunk the Credit of their Historians. One half of the Nation is always at Variance with the other half. I have met with People who assur'd me that the Duke of *Marlborough* was a Coward, and that Mr. *Pope* was a Fool; just as some Jesuits in *France* declare *Pascal* to have been a Man of little or no Genius; and some Jansenists affirm Father *Bourdaloüe* to have been a mere Babbler. The Jacobites consider *Mary* Queen of *Scots* as a pious Heroine, but those of an opposite Party look upon her as a Prostitute, an Adulteress, a Murtherer. Thus the *English* have Memorials of the several Reigns, but no such Thing as a History. There is indeed now living, one Mr. *Gordon*, (the Publick are oblig'd to him for a Translation of *Tacitus*) who is very capable of writing the History of his own Country, but *Rapin de Thoyras* got the Start of him. To conclude, in my Opinion, the *English* have not such good Historians as the *French*, have no such Thing as a real Tragedy, have several delightful Comedies, some wonderful Passages in certain of their Poems, and boast of Philosophers that are worthy of instructing Mankind. The *English* have reap'd very great Benefit from the Writers of our Nation, and therefore we ought, (since they have not scrupled to be in our Debt) to borrow from them. Both the *English* and we came after the *Italians*, who have been our In-structors in all the Arts, and whom we have surpass'd in some. I cannot determine which of the three Nations ought to be honour'd with the Palm; but happy the Writer who could display their various Merits.

LETTER XXIII.

ON THE

REGARD

That ought to be shown to

MEN OF LETTERS.

NEITHER the *English*, nor any other People have Foundations establish'd in favour of the polite Arts like those in *France*. There are Universities in most Countries, but 'tis in *France* only that we meet with so beneficial an Encouragement for Astronomy, and all Parts of the Mathematicks, for Physick, for Researches into Antiquity, for Painting, Sculpture and Architecture. *Lewis* the Fourteenth has immortaliz'd his Name by these several Foundations, and this Immortality did not cost him two hundred thousand Livres a Year.

I MUST confess that one of the Things I

very much wonder at, is, that as the Parliament of *Great-Britain* have promis'd a Reward of twenty thousand Pounds Sterling to any Person who may discover the Longitude, they should never have once thought to imitate *Lewis* the Fourteenth in his Munificence with regard to the Arts and Sciences.

MERIT indeed meets in *England* with Rewards of another kind, which redound more to the Honour of the Nation. The *English* have so great a Veneration for exalted Talents, that a Man of Merit in their Country is always sure of making his Fortune. Mr. *Addison* in *France* would have been elected a Member of one of the Academies, and, by the Credit of some Women, might have obtain'd a yearly Pension of twelve hundred Livres; or else might have been imprison'd in the *Bastile*, upon Pretence that certain Strokes in his Tragedy of *Cato* had been discover'd, which glanc'd at the Porter of some Man in Power. Mr. *Addison* was rais'd to the Post of Secretary of State in *England*. Sir *Isaac Newton* was made Warden of the Royal Mint. Mr. *Congreve* had a considerable * Employment. Mr. *Prior* was Plenipotentiary. Dr. *Swift* is Dean of St. *Patrick* in *Dublin*, and is more rever'd in *Ireland* than the Primate himself. The Religion which Mr. *Pope* professes excludes him indeed from Preferments of ev'ry kind, but then it did not prevent his gaining

* Secretary for *Jamaica*.

two hundred Thousand Livres by his excellent Translation of *Homer*. I my self saw a long Time in *France* the Author of * *Rhadamistus* ready to perish for Hunger: And the Son of one of the greatest Men† our Country ever gave Birth to, and who was beginning to run the noble Career which his Father had set him, would have been reduc'd to the Extremes of Misery, had he not been patroniz'd by Monsieur *Fagon*.

BUT the Circumstance which mostly encourages the Arts in *England*, is the great Veneration which is paid them. The Picture of the prime Minister hangs over the Chimney of his own Closet, but I have seen that of Mr. *Pope* in twenty Noblemens Houses. Sir *Isaac Newton* was rever'd in his Life-time, and had a due respect paid to him after his Death; the greatest Men in the Nation disputing who shou'd have the Honour of holding up his Pall. Go into *Westminster-Abbey*, and you'll find that what raises the Admiration of the Spectator is not the Mausoleums of the *English* Kings, but the Monuments which the Gratitude of the Nation has erected, to perpetuate the Memory of those illustrious Men who contributed to its Glory. We view their Statues in that Abbey in the same Manner, as those of *Sophocles*, *Plato* and other immortal Personages were view'd in *Athens*; and I am persuaded, that the bare Sight of those glorious Monuments has fir'd more than one

* Mr. *de Crebillon*.   † *Racine*.

Breast, and been the Occasion of their becoming great Men.

THE *English* have even been reproach'd with paying too extravagant Honours to mere Merit, and censured for interring the celebrated Actress Mrs. *Oldfield* in *Westminster-Abbey*, with almost the same Pomp as Sir *Isaac Newton*. Some pretend that the *English* had paid her these great Funeral Honours, purposely to make us more strongly sensible of the Barbarity and Injustice which they object to us, for having buried *Mademoiselle le Couvreur* ignominiously in the Fields.

BUT be assur'd from me, that the *English* were prompted by no other Principle, in burying Mrs. *Oldfield* in *Westminster-Abbey*, than their good Sense. They are far from being so ridiculous as to brand with Infamy an Art which has immortaliz'd an *Euripides* and a *Sophocles*; or to exclude from the Body of their Citizens a Sett of People whose Business is to set off with the utmost Grace of Speech and Action, those Pieces which the Nation is proud of.

UNDER the Reign of *Charles* the First, and in the Beginning of the Civil Wars rais'd by a Number of rigid Fanaticks, who at last were the Victims to it; a great many Pieces were publish'd against Theatrical and other Shews, which were attack'd with the greater Virulence, because that Monarch and his Queen, Daughter to *Henry* the Fourth of *France*, were passionately fond of them.

ONE Mr. *Prynne*, a Man of most furiously scrupulous Principles, who wou'd have thought himself damn'd had he wore a Cassock instead of a short Cloak, and have been glad to see one half of Mankind cut the other to Pieces for the Glory of God, and the *Propaganda Fide*; took it into his Head to write a most wretched Satyr against some pretty good Comedies, which were exhibited very innocently every Night before their Majesties. He quoted the Authority of the Rabbis, and some Passages from St. *Bonaventure*, to prove that the *Œdipus* of *Sophocles* was the Work of the evil Spirit; that *Terence* was excommunicated *ipso facto*; and added, that doubtless *Brutus*, who was a very severe Jansenist, assassinated *Julius Cæsar*, for no other Reason, but because he, who was *Pontifex Maximus*, presum'd to write a Tragedy the Subject of which was *Œdipus*. Lastly, he declar'd that all who frequented the Theatre were excommunicated, as they thereby renounc'd their Baptism. This was casting the highest Insult on the King and all the Royal Family; and as the *English* lov'd their Prince at that Time, they cou'd not bear to hear a Writer talk of excommunicating him, tho' they themselves afterwards cut his Head off. *Prynne* was summon'd to appear before the Star-Chamber; his wonderful Book, from which Father *Le Brun* stole his, was sentenc'd to be burnt by the Common Hangman, and himself to lose his Ears. His Tryal is now extant.

THE *Italians* are far from attempting to cast a Blemish on the Opera, or to excommunicate Signior *Senesino* or Signora *Cuzzoni*. With regard to my self, I cou'd presume to wish that the Magistrates wou'd suppress I know not what contemptible Pieces, written against the Stage. For when the *English* and *Italians* hear that we brand with the greatest Mark of Infamy an Art in which we excell; that we excommunicate Persons who receive Salaries from the King; that we condemn as impious a Spectacle exhibited in Convents and Monasteries; that we dishonour Sports in which *Lewis* the Fourteenth, and *Lewis* the Fifteenth perform'd as Actors; that we give the Title of the Devil's Works to Pieces which are receiv'd by Magistrates of the most severe Character, and represented before a virtuous Queen; when, I say, Foreigners are told of this insolent Authority, and this Gothic Rusticity which some presume to call Christian Severity; what an Idea must they entertain of our Nation? And how will it be possible for 'em to conceive, either that our Laws give a Sanction to an Art which is declar'd infamous, or that some Persons dare to stamp with Infamy an Art which receives a Sanction from the Laws, is rewarded by Kings, cultivated and encourag'd by the greatest Men, and admir'd by whole Nations? And that Father *Le*

Brun's impertinent Libel against the Stage, is seen in a Bookseller's Shop, standing the very next to the immortal Labours of *Racine*, of *Corneille*, of *Moliere*, &c.

LETTER XXIV.

ON THE

ROYAL SOCIETY

AND OTHER

ACADEMIES.

THE *English* had an Academy of Sciences many Years before us, but then it is not under such prudent Regulations as ours, the only Reason of which very possibly is, because it was founded before the Academy of *Paris*; for had it been founded after, it would very probably have adopted some of the sage Laws of the former, and improv'd upon others.

T w o Things, and those the most essential to Man, are wanting in the Royal Society of *London*, I mean Rewards and Laws. A Seat in the Academy at *Paris* is a small, but secure Fortune to a Geometrician or a Chymist; but this is so far from being the Case at *London*, that the several Members of the Royal Society are at a continual, tho' indeed small Expence. Any Man in *England* who declares himself a Lover of the Mathematicks and natural Philosophy, and expresses an Inclination to be a Member of the Royal Society, is immediately elected into it.* But in *France* 'tis not enough that a Man who aspires to the Honour of being a Member of the Academy, and of receiving the Royal Stipend, has a love for the Sciences; he must at the same Time be deeply skill'd in them; and is oblig'd to dispute the Seat with Competitors who are so much the more formidable as they are fir'd by a Principle of Glory, by Interest, by the Difficulty it self, and by that Inflexibility of Mind, which is generally found in those who devote themselves to that pertinacious Study, the Mathematicks.

THE Academy of Sciences is prudently confin'd to the Study of Nature, and, indeed, this is a Field spacious enough for fifty or three-score Persons to range in. That of *London* mixes indiscriminately Literature with Physicks: But methinks the founding an Academy merely for the polite Arts is more judicious, as it prevents Confusion, and the joining, in some Measure,

* The Reader will call to Mind that these Letters were written about 1728 or 30, since which Time the Names of the several Candidates are, by a Law of the Royal Society, posted up in it, in order that a Choice may be made of such Persons only as are qualified to be Members. The celebrated Mr. *de Fontenelle* had the Honour to pass thro' this *Ordeal.*

of Heterogeneals, such as a Dissertation on the Head-dresses of the *Roman* Ladies with an hundred or more new Curves.

As there is very little Order and Regularity in the Royal Society, and not the least Encouragement; and that the Academy of *Paris* is on a quite different Foot, 'tis no wonder that our Transactions are drawn up in a more just and beautiful Manner than those of the *English.* Soldiers who are under a regular Discipline, and besides well paid, must necessarily, at last, perform more glorious Atchievements than others who are mere Volunties. It must indeed be confess'd that the Royal Society boast their *Newton,* but then he did not owe his Knowledge and Discoveries to that Body; so far from it, that the latter were intelligible to very few of his Fellow-Members. A Genius like that of Sir *Isaac* belong'd to all the Academies in the World, because all had a thousand Things to learn of him.

T H E celebrated Dean *Swift* form'd a Design, in the latter End of the late Queen's Reign, to found an Academy for the *English* Tongue upon the Model of that of the *French.* This Project was promoted by the late Earl of *Oxford,* Lord High Treasurer, and much more by the Lord *Bolingbroke,* Secretary of State, who had the happy Talent of Speaking without Premeditation in the Parliament-house with as much Purity as Dean *Swift* writ in his Closet, and who would have been the Ornament and Protector of that Academy. Those only wou'd have been chosen Members of it, whose Works will last as long as the *English* Tongue, such as Dean *Swift*, Mr. *Prior*, whom we saw here invested with a publick Character, and whose Fame in *England* is equal to that of *La Fontaine* in *France*; Mr. *Pope* the English *Boileau*, Mr. *Congreve* who may be call'd their *Moliere*, and several other eminent Persons whose Names I have forgot; all these would have rais'd the Glory of that Body to a great Height even in it's Infancy. But Queen *Anne* being snatch'd suddenly from the World, the Whigs were resolv'd to ruin the Protectors of the intended Academy, a Circumstance that was of the most fatal Consequence to polite Literature. The Members of this Academy would have had a very great Advantage over those who first form'd that of the *French*, for *Swift, Prior, Congreve, Dryden, Pope, Addison, &c.* had fix'd the *English* Tongue by their Writings; whereas *Chapelain, Colletet, Cassaigne, Faret, Perrin, Cotin*, our first Academicians, were a Disgrace to their Country; and so much Ridicule is now attach'd to their very Names, that if an Author of some Genius in this Age had the Misfortune to be call'd *Chapelain* or *Cotin*, he would be under a Necessity of changing it.

ONE Circumstance, to which the *English* Academy should especially have attended, is, to have prescrib'd to themselves Occupations of a quite different kind from those with which our Academicians amuse themselves. A Wit of this Country ask'd me for the Memoirs of the *French* Academy. I answer'd, they have no Memoirs, but have printed threescore or fourscore Volumes in Quarto of Compliments. The Gentleman perus'd one or two of 'em, but without being able to understand the Style in which they were written, tho' he understood all our good Authors perfectly. All, says he, I see in these elegant Discourses is, that the Member elect having assur'd the Audience that his Predecessor was a great Man, that Cardinal *Richelieu* was a very great Man, that the Chancellor *Seguier* was a pretty great Man, that *Lewis* the Fourteenth was a more than great Man; the Director answers in the very same Strain, and adds, that the Member elect may also be a sort of great Man, and that himself, in Quality of Director, must also have some Share in this Greatness.

THE Cause why all these academical Discourses have unhappily done so little Honour to this Body is evident enough. *Vitium est temporis potiùs quam hominis.* (The Fault is owning to the Age rather than to particular Persons.) It grew up insensibly into a Custom for every Academician to repeat these Elogiums at his Reception; 'twas laid down as a kind of Law, that the Publick should be indulg'd from Time to Time the sullen Satisfaction of yawning over these Productions. If the Reason should afterwards be sought, why the greatest Genius's who have been incorporated into the Body have sometimes made the worst Speeches; I answer, that 'tis wholly owing to a strong Propension, the Gentlemen in Question had to shine, and to display a thread-bare, worn-out Subject in a new and uncommon Light. The Necessity of saying something, the Perplexity of having nothing to say, and a Desire of being witty, are three Circumstances which alone are capable of making even the greatest Writer ridiculous. These Gentlemen, not being able to strike out any new Thoughts, hunted after a new Play of Words, and deliver'd themselves without thinking at all; in like Manner as People who should seem to chew with great Eagerness, and make as tho' they were eating, at the same Time that they were just starv'd.

'T I S a Law in the *French* Academy to publish all those Discourses by which only they are known, but they should rather make a Law never to print any of them.

B U T the Academy of the *Belles Lettres* have a more prudent and more useful Object, which is, to present the Publick with a Collection of Transactions that abound with curious Researches and Critiques. These Transactions are already esteem'd by Foreigners; and it were only to be wish'd, that some Subjects in them had been more thoroughly examined, and that others had not been treated at all. As for In-stance, we should have been very well satisfied, had they omitted I know not what Dissertation on the Prerogative of the Right Hand over the Left; and some others, which tho' not publish'd under so ridiculous a Title, are yet written on Subjects that are almost as frivolous and silly.

THE Academy of Sciences, in such of their Researches as are of a more difficult kind and a more sensible Use, embrace the Knowledge of Nature and the Improvements of the Arts. We may presume that such profound, such uninterrupted Pursuits as these, such exact Calculations, such refin'd Discoveries, such extensive and exalted Views, will, at last, produce something that may prove of Advantage to the Universe. Hitherto, as we have observ'd together, the most useful Dis-coveries have been made in the most barbarous Times. One wou'd conclude, that the Business of the most enlightned Ages and the most learned Bodies, is, to argue and debate on Things which were invented by ignorant People. We know exactly the Angle which the Sail of a Ship is to make with the Keel, in order to its sailing better; and yet *Columbus* discover'd *America*, without having the least Idea of the Property of this Angle: However I am far from inferring from hence, that we are to confine our selves merely to a blind Practice, but happy it were, wou'd Naturalists and Geometricians unite, as much as possible, the Practice with the Theory.

STRANGE, but so it is, that those Things which reflect the greatest Honour on the human Mind, are frequently of the least Benefit to it! A Man who understands the four Fundamental Rules of Arithmetic, aided by a little good Sense, shall amass prodigious Wealth in Trade, shall become a Sir *Peter Delmé*, a Sir *Richard Hopkins*, a Sir *Gilbert Heathcot*, whilst a poor Algebraist spends his whole Life in searching for astonishing Properties and Relations in Numbers, which at the same time are of no manner of Use, and will not acquaint him with the Nature of Exchanges. This is very nearly the Case with most of the Arts; there is a certain Point, beyond which, all Researches serve to no other Purpose, than merely to delight an inquisitive Mind. Those ingenious and useless Truths may be compar'd to Stars, which, by being plac'd at too great a Distance, cannot afford us the least Light.

WITH regard to the *French* Academy, how great a Service would they do to Literature, to the Language, and the Nation, if, instead of publishing a set of Compliments annually, they would give us new Editions of the valuable Works written in the Age of *Lewis* the Fourteenth, purged from the several Errors of Diction which are crept into them. There are many of these Errors in *Corneille* and *Moliere*, but those in *La Fontaine* are very numerous. Such as could not be corrected, might at least be pointed out. By this Means, as all the *Europeans* read those Works, they would teach them our Language in its utmost Purity, which, by that Means, would be fix'd to a lasting Standard; and valuable *French* Books being then printed at the King's Expence, would prove one of the most glorious Monuments the Nation could boast. I have been told that *Boileau* formerly made this Proposal, and that it has since been revived by a * Gentleman eminent for his Genius, his fine Sense, and just Taste for Criticism; but this Thought has met with the Fate of many other useful Projects, of being applauded and neglected.

* *L'Abbe de Rothelin* of the *French* Academy.

F I N I S .

INDEX.

A.

I.

IMPULSION. A Term as little understood in Philosophy as that of Attraction, *pag.* 104.

INFINITES in Geometry. Carried by Sir *Isaac Newton* to a wonderful Length, *p.* 117, & *seq.*

INOCULATION. An artificial Method of communicating the Small-Pox, first brought from *Asia*. Origin of this Invention; Curious Relation how it was first introduc'd in *England*, *p.* 60. Effect it had in that Country, *p.* 61. Great Benefit it might produce in other Countries, especially in *France*, *p.* 62. The *Chinese* are said to have practis'd it for a long Course of Years, *p.* 63.

INVENTIONS. Several great Men have disputed for the Honour of various Inventions, *p.* 116.

L.

LEIBNITZ. Whether he invented *Fluxions*, *p.* 116.

LEWENHOECK. His Dispute with *Hartsoecher*, *p.* 116.

LIBERTY. Idoliz'd so much by the *English*, that they are even jealous of that of other Nations, *p.* 42. Foundation of their Liberties, *p.* 50. These examin'd, *p.* 51. & *seq.*

LOCKE (Mr.) His Character, *p.* 73. Idea of his Philosophy, *p.* 76, & *seq.* He is accus'd of a Design to destroy Religion, *p.* 78.

T.

TELESCOPES. One of a new kind invented by Sir *Isaac Newton, p.* 113.

THEATRES. The *English* had these before the *French, p.* 125.

THEE and THOU. The Quakers always use those Particles in speaking. Justification of that Form of Speech, *p.* 6. Example of a Discourse of this kind address'd to *Charles* II, *p.* 17.

THUANUS. A judicious Author even in his Style, *p.* 72.

TORIES. A powerful Party in *England*, the Counter-part to the Whigs, *p.* 28.

TRANSLATION. Several Passages of the most famous *English* Poets translated by Mr. *de Voltaire*. One of *Shakespear, p.* 129. of *Dryden, p.* 131. of the Earl of *Rochester, p.* 149. of *Waller, p.* 153. of Mr. *Pope, p.* 160. of the Lord ——, *p.* 145. Qualities necessary to form a good Translation, *p.* 130.

TRAGEDIES. Reflexions on the State of Tragedy in *England, p.* 132, *& seq.*

V.

VANBRUGH (Sir *John*) Author of several good Comedies, and an Architect. His Character and Epitaph, *p.* 139, was imprison'd in the *Bastile, ibid.*

VILLEQUIER (Duke of). Dies in the Flower of his Youth, *p.* 63.